INSPIRED
RUG-HOOKING
Turning Atlantic Canadian Life Into Art

DEANNE FITZPATRICK

NIMBUS
PUBLISHING

Nimbus Publishing Limited
3731 Mackintosh St, Halifax, NS B3K 5A5
(902) 455-4286   nimbus.ca

Printed and bound in Canada

Author photo: Katherine Hatheway
Design: Kate Westphal, Graphic Detail Inc.

Library and Archives Canada Cataloguing in Publication
        Fitzpatrick, Deanne
        Inspired rug-hooking : turning Atlantic Canadian life
        into art / Deanne Fitzpatrick.
        ISBN 978-1-55109-780-0
1. Rugs, Hooked—Atlantic Provinces. I. Title.
TT850.F583 2010   746.7'4   C2010-905142-4

We acknowledge the financial support of the Government of Canada through
the Book Publishing Industry Development Program (BPIDP) and the Canada
Council, and of the Province of Nova Scotia through the Department of
Tourism, Culture and Heritage for our publishing activities.

Acknowledgements

On a daily basis I rely on the people who help me in the studio so
that I can focus on hooking rugs and stringing words together.
Brenda Clarke, Gwen Kerr, Katherine Hatheway, Norma Milner,
Colleen Keagan, Lorna Davis, and Bill Hopper are all a beautiful
part of my studio life, and I thank them deeply. And thank you to
Kate Kennedy at Nimbus who helped me make this book so much
better.

*To Robert Mansour
who twenty-five years ago
first showed me the difference
between a painting
and a picture.*

CONTENTS

"The Words Between Us" is about friendship and the stories that flow between two people.

INTRODUCTION

Making rugs is not just a utilitarian practice; it is a personal journey. I believe that in making many rugs, or any other kind of art, you are constantly confronted with your powerlessness to be perfect, or to even be what you want to be, and your comfort with this imperfection makes you open and accepting of "less than-ness." You realize that you are a small part of something bigger. What you imagine and what comes out are different. My sister Joan is fond of saying, "it is what it is," in reference to all kinds of things. When you finish a mat, you realize "it is what it is." It might not be what you set out to create. Making mats can be humbling. It makes you search for ways of doing it better the next time, just like we do when we make mistakes in life.

Every mat I make is a failure in some way. Occasionally one goes far beyond my expectations and when I first take it off the frame, I think, "this is the one." Then I live with it and like a mate, no matter how wonderful it begins, I start to look at it critically, and I see the flaws, but I accept them as a natural consequence of being human, or in this case, of being made by hand. There is no perfection, only love and acceptance. There is the glory of being able to be better if I keep working at it, of understanding that there is strength in acknowledging my own weaknesses. For how can one look at the flaws of another, or of something made with the hands, and not be confronted with their own inherent flaws?

Last summer I visited Marie Helene Allain, a nun who is also a sculptor. She was showing me her abstract stone sculptures. A delicately boned woman, with abnormally strong hands, she chisels away at rock to bring out the form she sees. She has been a sculptor since shortly after she joined the convent. Thinking that she would have to choose between the two, she visited her Mother Superior to tell her that she was torn, and needed to make art all the time, and

I leave this sign up in my studio to remind me of the importance of ideas, of thinking things through.

could not commit to be a teaching sister. She giggled when she told me that her Mother Superior said, "It will be okay. After all, Marie Allain, we are not in it for the money." For over forty years her order has supported her decision to be an artist. She, of course, has contributed much to the order for being allowed to be herself. It is true for all of us: when we are allowed to be ourselves, we have more to offer others. Her sculpture was very moving. I asked her, artist to artist: "Do you still get down on your knees to pray?" I was curious, not having really spent much time with a nun as a peer before. She said, "Oh well, I rarely get down on my knees to pray, but I pray all the time with my work." She said she felt that whether you believed in God or not, making things, making art, was an act of faith. "To work," she said, "is to pray."

Making things is a humbling experience whatever way you see it. Putting your spirit into something and having it not be everything you want it to be is what creation is all about. As perfect as your children might be, they are never exactly what you expected, and the only real love that you can give them as a parent is to fully accept them as they are. My neighbour and walking buddy Rosemary says, "Deanne, they come out with their own souls." Like your children, your artwork, whatever that might be, also has its own spirit, and in loving your work, and respecting that it is not perfect, you accept yourself, your own soul, your own spirit. Your real work will come through you. Perhaps it will emerge even in spite of you, if you let it.

Our smallness is only reflected to ourselves in our work. It is not reflected to everyone. Others cannot see the weaknesses and mistakes we see. To others it may look perfect, even beautiful. As an artist, or a craftsperson, you don't need to be perfectly pleased with something for it to be perfect. Make it, finish it, give the community a chance to breathe it in.

Every morning, after I have eaten breakfast and my tea has steeped for fifteen minutes, to the point that it is strong and black and only slightly hot, I go to the frame like you would to a desk that has all your favourite papers and books on it. I go to it religiously, but, unlike Sister Marie Allain, there are only some times I am able to make it a meditation or a prayer. I have read, and I have felt, that when you are creating you can get closer to God or whoever you think made this beautiful place, where every leaf and every tiny creature has a structure that is intricate and complex and beautiful. You come to understand, as a mat-maker especially, that the world is created in patterns, with rhythm and beauty. This understanding comes from making rugs, because their creation is a meditation and through it you come to understand yourself and the world around you.

"Stay Inspired"

CHAPTER 1

Beauty by Design

Finding Beauty

Beauty is not always captured the first time you see something. Real beauty sometimes deepens as you get to know something better. I think of this when I think about how my relationship with the Tantramar Marsh has grown after living in Amherst for twenty-six years. The marsh— acres and acres of field and scrub and brush separating Nova Scotia from New Brunswick—looks like a barren when you first come to it. It is not an automatic "Isn't that beautiful." The first time I saw it, with its big radio towers and empty, hollow grey barns, I thought "wasteland." I was a teenager moving here from Newfoundland, where beauty was big and dramatic. The ocean roared at me all day long and told me to be good, to be careful, and to pay attention to it. The marsh on the other hand just lay there, baring its back quietly, waiting to see if I would notice.

It took me years to notice, but I did. It began with our friends Jill and Art who had a sheep farm in Fort Lawrence. We left the farm one morning in hip waders and headed down to pick cranberries growing in water. We spent all day in the frigid waters, with cattails and marsh grass hiding us from each other, and came home with ten pounds of wild cranberries. It was the first time I saw what the marsh had to give. That day on that flat, low landscape I could see for miles around. I saw how the marsh, not the town, was really at the centre of things.

I have had some lovely moments on the marsh. Walking on the marsh, and coming up over an Acadian dyke to see how the water meets the shore, I first learned the true colours of the Bay of Fundy. I'll never forget the dramatic surprise that the bay was so close as I walked up the small hill of the dyke and found that that particular dyke was the last fortress between the water and the hayfields of the marsh. Purple hues, laid over a river of chocolate, glistened, and I saw that at certain points, brown and mauve were really the same colour. I was taken aback by the beauty and suddenness of the empty bay at low tide. It was a study in brown, and since seeing it I have come to understand that colour differently. I now see that brown and mauve belong together, and that they should be met with blue.

I have lain on the dykes at Fort Beausejour with my head on my husband's chest, and listened to the sound of the train in the distance. On a warm summer day I would lie there waiting for the sound of a whistle so that I could become a part of a quintessential Canadian picture, long train winding in the distance, cutting across the wide open landscape. At moments like those I felt like I could lie there forever basking in the warmth.

History stands up to meet you on the dykes. It is hard not to think of the Acadians who built those dykes through backbreaking labour as you, generations later, lie upon them in peace and comfort. You can imagine people trying to carve out lives, eking out an existence on these wind-filled flats.

The marsh makes you feel like you know where you are when you do not. One early summer day I got lost on the marsh dykes with my friend Rosemary. We missed a path because on the marsh, every path looks the same. After walking for a couple of hours, we ended up behind a couple of farms in west Amherst and had to climb over barbed-wire fences and walk through cow fields to get back to the car. Getting lost on the marsh is as easy as getting lost in the woods.

Once I took a boat ride down marsh creeks that were covered in yellow gold lilies and their pads. All of a sudden the unlikely creek was a Monet painting. There it was, water lilies and grass, all sparkling

The CBC towers on the Tantramar marsh are a beacon to me. They tell me I am nearly home.

in the sunlight. I picked some of the lilies, brought them home in a big five-gallon bucket, and delicately placed them in a bowl on my kitchen table. But they didn't look like they belonged. Their beauty was conditional on being where they belonged. I feel like that myself. For me beauty is about belonging. When I travel, I long for home, my wool, my books and papers, and my sense of displacement always makes me feel uncertain and lost. I wilt a little, like the water lilies, wishing I were home.

Snowshoeing across the Eddy Road one winter towards Fort Lawrence, a Great Blue Heron suddenly flung itself up out of a creek, surprising me with its grey-blue wings against the snow. For whatever natural reason, this one did not leave that winter. It found a home on the marsh. I hope it survived the winter. Other days, hawks have swooped down at me and eagles have soared above me. These moments on the Tantramar are just bits of beauty, moments of a life lived near a lovely place. I remember them like scenes from a lovely film in which I am a character. They occupy my mind and lure me back to the marsh again and again. Sometimes on a walk through town I dash out the Eddy Road for five minutes just to see what is on the marsh and to listen to grass and brush.

These marsh vignettes make me feel that beauty is enough of a reason to make art. I do question that statement sometimes when I begin to compare myself with other artists or wonder if I'm going in the right direction with my work. For some artists, making beautiful art is a cop-out—they feel that art should be more than beauty, that prettiness is the equivalent of pettiness in art. But for me, when I am struggling with the question of whether beauty is enough, the solution is to make something beautiful, and *then* see how I feel. Never once have I made a mat that I found to be beautiful and wondered if it had been a waste of time. If a rug is beautiful, it is enough.

I rarely hook the Tantramar Marsh in a literal way, but it inspires all kinds of other mats for me. Lying there on the dykes inspires mats about love. Remembering how it must have been to build those dykes inspires mats about hard work. The grasses and brush of the marsh turn up in my field rugs.

Never once have I made a mat that I found to be beautiful and wondered if it had been a waste of time.

Making art is not always a direct relationship to what you see. It is more about internalizing what you see, and then seeing how it emerges. It is about taking in one thing, and sending out another. Art is about transformation. For me it is about seeing the ordinary and finding the beautiful. More than anything I want to make rugs that are beautiful. Trite as that may be to some, it makes sense to me, because I believe there is meaning in beauty, and that in life we seek beauty as much as anything.

Creating Beauty: How to Design Rugs

There are many elements of good rug design. It is about putting things together in a way that pleases the eye, so that when you look upon something there is a satisfaction and a comfort in what you see. It is pleasing and interesting to the eye. It can be about understanding order, balance, sensibility, and colour.

Rug design can but does not always involve drawing. You can design something by planning the layout of it, which elements go where, without ever drawing it. You can have someone else do the drawing for you, and still be the designer. Drawing adds to your ability to design because it allows you to sketch freely, and build confidence in your ability. Drawing is definitely a skill that can be developed. It does not rely solely on talent. Betty Edwards proved this in her famous book *Drawing on the Right Side of the Brain*. With practice and skill development, people who could not draw well were able to become accurate and representational in their drawing. I like to tell people, "Be thankful if you can't draw a straight line." Drawing does not require you to be able to draw a straight line. In rug hooking, you'll only use them for geometrics and for that you can use a ruler. What I like to tell people is to hold the pencil loosely. Often we grab our pencil like it is trying to escape our hands. Hold the pencil as if it belongs in

When I read, ideas and images come to mind, so I am constantly seeking out books, new and old.

your hand. Do not compare your drawings to those of others. Your drawings will look different from others' not only because they may have more or less skill but because you see things differently. Accept that you have your own view, your own way of seeing, and be grateful for that. It is the stuff that art is made of.

Creativity is the essential part of good rug design. Some see creativity as a gift from the gods endowed upon a certain few. This belief can be a kind of defence for people who have not explored their creative side. They think that because they didn't get to drink the nectar, they can't be expected to create. There is nothing further from the truth. Creativity can be developed in people. It comes from a way of being, from nurturing and developing a childlike approach to life. Eugene Ionesco pondered the question: If you act like an artist will you become an artist? I believe for certain that if you act like an artist you will become an artist. What artists do, essentially, is make stuff. If you make stuff day in, day out, drawing

An honest look at my dye kitchen: a lovely mess in simple form

upon your own spirit to do so, you will become an artist. Artists are not part of a secret society. Rather they are often curious people who play with ideas and spend time making things. Some people have a natural abundance of creativity. They ooze it. For others it is something that is developed. I believe that everyone has some ability to design, draw, and create, no matter how limited, and that these are all skills that can be enhanced through practice.

Creativity is enhanced by the way you live, and the approach with which you meet your life. It requires openness and a willingness to explore; the rest will fall into place. Becoming an artist with that type of creativity requires a commitment of time and energy. To be an artist you must make the work.

Many of us have fears about our own creativity. We have built stone walls around our creativity through the way we have talked to and about ourselves over the years. We have listened when people around us told us we were not creative. Over the years we have become accustomed to the idea that we are not creative or cannot draw. (I notice how people who are encouraged creatively, told by their friends and relatives how creative they are, blossom and develop. The encouragement gives them courage.) You might want to think about what kinds of fears you have around your own creativity. Are you afraid to fail, to discover that you have little to express? Are you worried what others will think of your creative effort? Are you afraid of the difficult parts of yourself you may discover as you delve into your creativity? Are you scared of wasting time, of using your energy only to find that the results are much less than what you had hoped for?

The truth is that all artists experience fear, but they do not let it limit them. They engage their fears and move ahead. Time can be wasted, and failure on some level is inevitable for all of us. If you are going to be successful in designing your own work you need to be prepared for both of these things. You will fail to meet your expectations. You will waste some time. Most importantly you will learn things from lollygagging, and from sorrowful, horrible mats, that you could never learn from the just-so-sweet little tea cozy you hooked for your sister. The sweet little tea cozies are "cute." They need to be done, no doubt about it. They are a great exercise in not taking yourself too seriously. They matter in a different way. But also take some risks on some good-sized mats and see what you have to learn from them.

The terrible creative failures will teach you what not to do, and you can carry those "what not to do" rules into every future project. There is a critical juncture in many creative projects where you have the opportunity to try

I notice how people who are encouraged creatively, told by their friends and relatives how creative they are, blossom and develop.

it the safe way, or to try it a new way. The safe way is useful; you may have learned it from past risks that did not work out. You can take the safe way and push it a little. Most artists develop this way, slowly pushing their boundaries in ways that see them through their work. They grow slowly, sensibly, safely. But every once in a while artists make the leap and approach something in a new way. The new way, as often as not, might be a waste of valuable time and expensive resources, but artists know that if they try it sometimes they'll be rewarded with that powerful and exciting feeling in their chest that makes their heart beat, that re-energizes them. It is worth the risk. Sometimes, in a large rug that seems like an overall failure, there is one element that worked, and learning that one thing makes the whole process worth the effort.

In rug design there is no sense in striving for perfection. We are trying to translate a vision from our heads and turn it into something real. When we struggle for perfection, we make it difficult to take the next step. Recently I did a short workshop on mermaids, and a couple of the participants admitted to being perfectionists. Every time they added a colour, or had to make a choice about the way to hook the colour into the tail of the mermaid, they struggled because they did not want to fail. Finally I said, "What if you do fail? What will you have lost? It will be three hours of trying." They needed to let go of their personalities for a little while and get lost in the story of the mermaid they were making. Our struggle must be to allow our hands to have a part in the making, as we develop and adapt our vision. We need to respect that our hands have input and that as the idea flows from our minds, through our hands, it will develop and change. There is no direct process for getting an idea straight from your head to the paper, or to a rug. You are affected by the materials available to you, your skills and abilities, the knowledge in the community around you, and countless other things. The first rug I ever designed turned out to be completely different than what I had set out to do. It had to be. I needed to accept what I liked about it, learn from the rest of it, and move on. Imagine if in life we let our mistakes freeze us from making other decisions, from moving forward. Art is life, and life is art. Playful dedication will lead to success, just as it does in work or business, or any other part of life. If you commit to designing your own rugs, and keep at it, they will get better.

CHOOSING AND PREPARING A BACKING

I have always preferred burlap as a backing for my rugs, but there are many different choices available. The backing you choose should be comfortable to work with and should be woven so that you can pull the wool loops up through the backing without stress or strain on your hand. There is nothing so uncomfortable as trying to pull up thick wool through tightly woven backing. As well, trying to hook a fine yarn through a loosely woven backing will only lead to trouble. The backing you choose should work well with the thickness and width of wool you are using. You should be able to hook the wool strips easily and with pleasure as you relax and work on your project.

Primitive burlap has a loose weave and is the traditional choice of the old-fashioned rug-makers. It is excellent for hauling up thick cloths and wide cuts. Traditional Scottish burlap is woven in an even grid and is good for finer cuts and lighter weights of cloth. Open weave Scottish burlap is an excellent choice for hooking wider cuts and thicker

Webster's Dictionary defines *lollygag* as "to fool around." Lollygagging is the root of all creativity, and fooling around is what we need to do. We need to play. We need to lose ourselves in our surroundings. We need to be open to new ideas. What appears to be a genuine waste of time is really the generative part of creativity. Recently I told a friend I needed to learn something new. She said the nicest thing to me. She said, "Your brain is so nice and stretchy." Automatically I thought of this little mass in my head doing its own kind of yoga. Think of your brain as something that needs its own yoga. Taking a long drive in the country, or finding a new experience, new ways to play, makes your brain more stretchy, and a nice stretchy brain is important for all kinds of reasons, especially as we age. It is essential to change up your routine a little, offer your mind new ideas, and choose new toys to play with.

Though creativity is the solid base of good design, this creative energy needs to be applied to the important elements of good rug design. Composition is one of these elements and it is about what goes where in your design. All parts of a good design seem to be in the right place. We know when we see great design, so it is important to start evaluating what we think works when we see it. What about it is so pleasing? What do we like? Knowing what you like is a good first step, because it allows you to emulate a little until you find your own voice. In good composition, you want to create a sense of wholeness throughout the mat, so that it feels like one piece of

wools as it is designed especially for this. Monks' cloth is preferred by some people because it is 100 percent cotton and does not have the scratchy feeling of burlap. It is stretchier than burlap or linen, wears well, and makes a good rug backing. Linen is the premium rug backing. It is a strong backing that wears well and stands the test of time. I have used all types of backing and found they each have their strengths and weaknesses.

Your backing should be relatively new. Do not use backings that have been stored for years, as they may be weak and holes will appear seemingly out of nowhere. Make sure your backing is strong and in good condition as it is the foundation of the rug you are making. Also keep your backing taut when you put it on the frame and as you continue to hook, as this will make the hooking easier and more comfortable.

artwork. Our eyes should want to take in the image as a whole, and then be drawn to different points of interest.

Good design usually needs a focal point, or some point of interest that draws the viewer in. There are many ways of adding interest to your composition. For example, omit or truncate things. Show only half, or part of objects. Points of interest are often created by adding people, buildings, shrubbery, trees, or other objects at key places in the design. I rely on intuition here, as in all parts of design. Intuition is built by studying good design, and by designing yourself. You do not have to hook every mat you design. I have thousands of designs in sketchbooks that I will never get to, but each of those designs has contributed something to the overall look of every mat I have made. All those scribbles, all that laying out and moving around of objects and figures, were exercises in composition. You do not have to hook every one you create, but each one you create will add to the one that you finally do hook.

Balance is an important element in composition. You do not want to make one side too heavy, the other too light. Every shape, colour, and texture has weight to it, and as you add them you change the balance of the design. This does not mean that every rug should hang like the scales of justice, it only means that you should look at your design and consider whether you have leaned too heavily on any one area of your mat. Is there too much of one colour, texture, or design in one part of the rug, and not enough in some of the other parts?

Perspective is another important part of composition. It is a simple concept, meaning that the smaller an item is, the further away it appears. It is a technique that you develop only through learning to draw well. Start noticing the size of the trees in the foreground and the size of the trees in the background as you drive down the road, and perspective will become very clear. For example, in "Two Madonnas of Church Street" it is okay for the women to appear larger than the houses because they are in the foreground.

There are a few general rules I rely on and rarely break. I avoid horizontal lines across the middle of the rug, because it divides the

"Two Madonnas of Church Street." One day when
walking into town I saw Donna Gibson and Donna
Morris carrying laundry and singing spirituals. I
had them come to my house later so I could draw them.

design in half and distracts a viewer from being able to see the mat as a whole. I often rely on the rule of thirds, for foreground, middle ground, and background, dividing the design into three distinct areas for landscapes. This adds a nice sense of balance to most designs. I eyeball the divide, of course, making it approximately a third, a third, and a third. I would never measure because I want it have a natural feeling.

Designers often suggest that you use odd numbers for groupings. So groups of threes or fives are preferable to groups of twos and fours. These of course are general rules, and we know that rules are made for breaking, especially when it comes to art and design. They are a great way to get you off and running, but relying on them in a habitual way means that your work will not develop. The set of three flowers in the corner (opposite) is a good example of this, and of how positioning an item can lend a sense of balance.

The sketchbook is the essential tool. Without it you will continue to draw a cat the way you did in grade six.

Make sure you have a good cache of design tools. You'll need pencils, a great sharpener, fine ink pens, a ruler, a yardstick, and a t-square. Get yourself a metal ruler and yardstick as they are less likely to have a warp and will keep your outside edges straighter. I bought myself the old-fashioned classroom pencil sharpener that screws into the wall and holds all the shavings. The whirling sound of my hand turning the crank puts me in the mood to draw with my nice sharp pencil. Perhaps it is nostalgia, but I have found it works the best.

The sketchbook is the essential tool. Without it you will continue to draw a cat the way you did in grade six. It is the place to collect your thoughts and ideas. You can write in it and draw in it. You can paste bits of good stuff in it that you have lying around: postcards, fabric, magazine articles, pictures. I always tell people to buy the one that looks too good for them to draw in and then to fill it, just to put it in its place. I like to make sure that it is perfect-bound (like a regular book) but done so that it opens flat, and I find that you are most likely to find this style in art stores. I don't like to have to press or hold the book open because this means I am not as free to draw.

I really enjoyed looking through the notebooks of Leonardo da Vinci, one of the most famous designers and artists of all time. The notebooks showed how diverse he was. He played with so many types of art. He was interested in drawing, architecture, sculpture, and engineering. He seemed to have an insatiable curiosity. In his early working life he was not only an artist but also acted as court organizer for the ruler of Milan, Lodovico Sforza. He organized parades, designed costumes, and was a musician and storyteller. He also designed weaponry for Sforza. Da Vinci always had a notebook with him. (If everyone always had pen and paper at their side, so many ideas would be documented instead of lost to us.) He was not educated, yet he wrote on philosophy, morality, ethics, and countless other subjects. He drew constantly. When he died in 1519 at the age of sixty-seven he left five thousand pages of notes to his assistant. Undoubtedly these notes are responsible for some of the fame he has received. Your notebooks or sketchbooks will be a valuable resource to you as you continue to make art. Da Vinci also valued time away from an idea or project, and may have been quite comfortable with lollygagging himself. In my studio I keep a quote from him pasted to the wall behind an old antique picture frame. It reads: "It will be useful too if he quit work often and take some relaxation; judgment will

I like how these plants emerge from the corner. I find parts or elements of things more interesting than the whole thing sometimes.

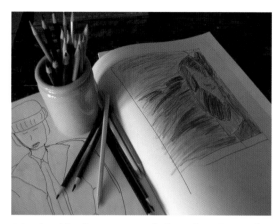

My sketchbooks are a record of my thoughts and ideas, telling me how I saw things at a certain time.

be clearer upon his return. Too great application and sitting still is sometimes the cause of great errors."

Ideas pop in and out of our heads. Just because we think something does not mean we will remember it. I keep a 25-cent lined notebook and a pen with me most of the time. If I get an idea, I jot it down. Truthfully, many of these ideas never get used, but occasionally one of them does, or they get blended with another idea and redeveloped. To me, there is nothing more beautiful than an idea. They are exquisite things, and too valuable to toss away. Ideas are not created out of thin air; they are so often the result of blending two existing thoughts together to create a new one. Ideas are meant to grow and develop and expand. It is perfectly natural that an idea could become completely unidentifiable from the original thought that led to it. Don't be inhibited by the fact that something has been done before; nearly everything has. Ask what you can add to it, what is in your experience that can enrich the idea. General ideas do not belong to anyone. Laundry on the line does not belong to any one artist, nor does a dog sitting in a chair. Play with ideas, making them your own, so they can become your originals and speak of you.

I do save all my sketchbooks and notebooks, and sometimes when I am not feeling so juicy and creative, I just make myself a cup of tea and go over them. It shows me how far I have come in my designs, but sometimes it also gets me back to good stuff I have left behind. I sometimes find a great design that I had forgotten about, or I see the roots of the design of the rugs I have recently made. If you are going to bother keeping account of your thoughts and ideas, then it is also good to take the time to review them once in a while. Savour what you have already done, what you have already gathered.

Finding inspiration becomes a more difficult part of rug design the further you are into your art-making. Initially you think there is an endless source of ideas for mats, but as you go along, and try many of them, the list sometimes starts to appear shorter. We do not always feel perfectly inspired, so staying inspired takes a little effort sometimes. I believe it is difficult to find inspiration if your surroundings are an utter mess. There is beauty in a mess, no doubt, but it can be harder to see. Make sure your surroundings are comfortable and somewhat organized. The idea that chaos and art go hand in hand is a fallacy for many people. I have always needed to surround myself with beauty, and for me that requires some order. I have discovered that often when I travel, I miss the sensibility that I have created around my house. I miss my bits of paper, my books, my sense of order, and the things I find beautiful. Those things are not fancy important things, but they are the beauty I have created for myself, and I lament for the comfort it offers me.

Accept that you have your own view, your own way of seeing, and be grateful for that. It is the stuff that art is made of.

To stay inspired I search out good ideas and I try to find out about the people who come up with them. I read good books. I don't create too many rules for myself. I nearly always finish my rugs so I can be inspired by my own work, but on a rare occasion I do let go of a project that I cannot seem to finish, because at a certain point it feels like it holds me back. I notice what I like, paying attention to my physical and emotional responses to colour and beauty. I try to take note and understand what I like about a thing. I try to connect with myself when I have an emotional response to something, to pay attention to and understand my feelings.

I sometimes go out on sketching expeditions to find inspiration. If you want, invite a friend over to go sketching with you. Pack a lunch and make a day of it. I also use my sketchbook to write in. Sometimes amidst a bunch of drawings I find some idea or notes to myself. Sometimes I annotate my drawings so that I will better remember the image that captivated me at a certain moment. These notes clarify in my mind just what I saw. I have a bunch of journals and at times I write, write, write, not for any other reason than to write. I keep an inspiration book, and a bulletin board full of bits of beauty. A shell, a stone, a bit of weathered bone, or a fossil laid on a shelf all embellish my life. They remind me of the beauty found in the absence of raucous colour. These things rely on the strength of form, sculptural beauty. Most artists I know collect bits of inspiration, and from these bits ideas develop. When I walk or hike I collect the interesting bits underfoot and return them to the studio with me. I also use this walking time to meditate or contemplate, as a time to soften my mind and my breathing. I see it as a time to be. Ideas come and go on these walks and I don't worry about them. It is a rare time without my notebook.

Take it easy on yourself. Make friends with a book, and sit for a while. I always try to rest instead of running myself ragged. One of the feelings I hate is the feeling of being rushed, so I try to avoid it. I think the notion of the selfish or self-centred artist is partly true, at least when it comes to time. We want time to draw, to design, to hook rugs. I try not to over-commit myself, which means I often say no so that I have the time to create. Part of creating for me is reading and resting, walking, and enjoying my life. A long-time friend once told me you can just say "Sorry, I can't make it," and that is enough of a reason for not doing something. I have found it easy to say no

TRANSFERRING PATTERNS

The first step in transferring a pattern is to have it enlarged on a photocopier to the size of rug you would like to create. This will usually involve taping together several pieces of 11-by-17-inch paper to reconstruct the pattern. You can transfer that pattern onto the backing of your choice using red dot tracer, which is available at craft supply stores. You simply lay the red dot tracer over the pattern and trace it with a black permanent marker. You can then lay the red dot tracer on your preferred backing and trace it again with the marker. The marker will seep through onto your new backing. When you are finished tracing, you can touch up your design by going over the pattern on the new backing with your marker. (You can also use wedding tulle, from fabric stores, as a transfer fabric.)

because I have a passion for what I do. It calls me and I am compelled to answer it.

Designing is about making time for art and creativity in your life. You can start as simply as you might like, with a rug of circles or squares, and get the process of creating your own designs rolling. Your level of commitment to sketching, drawing, and studying and practicing the elements of composition will determine how far you develop your own rugs as art. Know, though, that anyone can be an artist—you just need to act like one.

"Coral Cove." Houses remain one of the most important elements in my rugs. I love the feeling of home, and am inspired by it again and again.

House and Home

On Seven Acres

Over twenty years ago I moved five minutes outside of Amherst into an old farmhouse on seven acres of land. Two acres were spruce woods. There was a huge garden with a small plastic greenhouse that still stands. We came upon the house because there was an auction there and our friend Gary Bainbridge was going. He asked Robert, "Did you want me to get you anything?" Robert said, "Maybe the house. Ask about it." He did, and they said to call. When Robert called, Opal Chappell, who with her husband, Lawrence, had run a root-vegetable farm on the place for forty years, said she would be interested in talking and we could come visit. A week or so later on an early summer evening Robert and I and my little niece Kathleen took a drive out to visit Opal and have a look at the house. In the early evening light, Opal picked an orange off a small tree that she had grown in the little greenhouse and gave it to our seven-year-old niece. Opal had small old hands and I can still see them holding the orange against the light coming in through the greenhouse. We sat in the kitchen and talked under the dark wood slatted ceiling that remains there today. We did not talk about money but about the place. Robert and Opal's daughter Barb worked out the finances in the coming weeks. Opal said she wanted one last summer on the place and we could take it in September. We agreed.

The place has been good to us, and we to it. We keep a big unruly garden that is bordered by Russian Mammoth sunflowers that turn from grand dames in the summer to wilted and trembling old ladies

I have camouflaged the old plastic greenhouse with a grapevine. It remains, though it might blow away in a good wind.

by the end of winter. Nevertheless they stand through the strong winds of February and March and remain until I need to uproot them in June and plant their sisters to begin again. The property is plain, but it has become my muse, because I am charmed by what is plain in life more than I am charmed by the grand and the pretty. There is an untended apple orchard that blooms pink and white in late May, and in June a carpet of purple creeping Jenny lays a path through its twisted trunks to a skating pond that my husband dug out a few years ago. In the summer sometimes I take a blanket and lie upon the hill that overlooks the house. About five years ago my husband started mowing the big field, and for a few years, until the kids grew out of it, four or five families came over and played baseball on Wednesday nights. We have planted grape vines that now nearly cover the old greenhouse, and this year there were heaps of raspberries and strawberries in the garden. I would pick strawberries into a green and white speckled bowl, and leave them on the kitchen table to eat. Next year it could be beans. We take what comes.

In the winter when I snowshoe in the bit of woods I come out surprised to see the points and pitches of the roof, and the clean straight back of the house itself. This year, my neighbour Jan Boiduk has cut a trail through her woods that connects with my little trail, and told me I am free to use it. Her grandfather owned 192 acres, and she still lives on it. That's rural life. When we beat a path through the branches laden with snow this morning she said, "I feel like I am going into Narnia," and we were, in a way. Snow transforms this place, covering up its imperfections, and makes me feel as if I were in a magical place. From the edge of the woods I can see our small grey barn with its weathered shingles. It holds the winter's wood, and my wool, both things very dear. Alongside it a few spruce have sprung up wildly and carelessly as an old elm struggles year after year to make it.

There is nothing grand about this place. It does not overlook the ocean, or have huge sweeping windows, though there is a small river that winds below the neighbour's and if there are three days of rain it swells and floods Fage's field. It is not a particularly beautiful place but it is a place of our own, and in living with it I have come to understand the quality of the land, the richness of the soil. Its simplicity and ruggedness are characteristics that I value, ones that have charmed me and made me stay. This place does not tell me any lies about itself; there is no air of mystery. It is just a place and it has grown on me.

We dug a pond a few years ago. My neighbour Wayne Landry said, "Water brings life," and creatures gather there now.

The house itself is over 170 years old. From the basement you can see the timbers that built it. In the attic there are places where it is pegged together. You can roll balls down hills in some rooms but basically it feels straight and tight. We have tended to it faithfully, bringing it towards a new generation. We have looked after all of its needs and some of our own while preserving the four rooms, maintaining the traditional Georgian bones of the house. There are things about a farmhouse that was built for life in the 1840s that you would not choose for life today, but the truth is the few things it offers less of, like outlets for TVs and computers, are the same things that we can do with less of. It is a good house and it meets the needs of a family while at the same time reminding me that granite countertops and slick, even floors are not necessary, or even really that important. The house shows me that I will pass through it like

Both of these rugs, "Royal Sea of Blue" and "Looking out to Sea," are really about the house I spent my childhood in, overlooking Placentia Bay. I loved that home as well as the one I live in now.

the many families did before me, that I am impermanent, and I will slip in and out of its doors for forty years if I am lucky and then other lives will fill it after I have finished with it. Old houses hold stories of families and generations in their walls, but they hold them like secrets, and very little is ever told out of turn. When we hauled down the old walls in the back studio a small set of yellow airplane wings with red tips fell out. My son was just a boy, and it was a reminder to me that other little boys had played here before. In those airplane wings I saw the shortness, the sweetness, the fragility of life. My son is now nearly a man, and those wings hang in my studio, a reminder of time flying before my eyes. I also found the top of a wooden rake, a reminder that this was once a working farm, part of a land grant that went all the way to the River Philip in Oxford, nearly twenty miles away. The upstairs studio where I now work was an unfinished loft that held a set of bunks for itinerant farm hands who came and stayed while the crops were brought in. When we first moved in it was all grey

"Praise to the Sky." My rugs of houses are picturesque, but when I hook them I imagine the houses as containers for lives, not just pretty scenes.

unfinished barn boards and on the door between the two rooms of the upstairs loft was a scrap of paper that said "barn dance" in a woman's handwriting. This is a house with a history, and my life here is just the living history.

The living history that happens in this plain but privately picturesque place is not perfect. Plaster walls survive slamming doors, and you cannot see the stomping feet in the old pine steps of the staircase. We are not the first family who has shouted at each other between the walls or walked out into the evening disgusted. The four separate rooms upstairs and down serve us well; all four of us (me, my husband, and our son and daughter) are people who benefit from time alone, and require it to live with each other.

Part of this place being my muse is the people who live nearby. We have neighbours across the road, Owen and Shirley, who also keep five or six acres and a garden. I watch them from my kitchen window as their winter wood arrives in eight-foot lengths and they work together for days to cut and split and pile it for their furnace. I

"Three Window House" is a simply shaped house, defined by bright strong colours for the trim and sides.

see Owen walk around and tend his garden in a big straw hat. He'll haul the remnants of the plants that are finished over to the woods on the edge of his property in a wheelbarrow, wearing a white shirt, his thin shoulders shadowed by that straw hat. It is not a get-up or a costume. He is the real thing. Shirley shines in an old lime-green ski jacket from the seventies, brilliant against the solemn natural colours of the woodpile. In the evening I'll look out my kitchen window to see them sitting against their barn in a white wooden swing, the kind that glides back and forth. Once they looked so beautiful I hooked them a small rug of the two of them working on the woodpile. A few years later when I was visiting, Shirley told me she kept it good in the closet and brought it out to show. I laughed. Just like David Alan Coe said, "If that ain't country you can kiss my ass." There is little I like better than the truth, and no one I like better than people who tell the truth. If they like that rug in the closet, I am fine with that.

For years Fred Clarke lived a minute or two up the road from me. I barely knew him but I knew his red suspenders, the shape of his belly, and the way his pants came down narrow to the tips of his boots. I knew his stoop as he bent to reach into his rural mailbox across the road from his house. I knew the nod of his head as I walked past but I can honestly say I never knew the man who lived at the Y in the road. Yet, when he died last year I missed the familiarity of his presence. He was part of the life around my place. I know the movements and gestures of the people who live around me. I watch them, not out of nosiness, but just because I find gesture and habit interesting and picturesque.

There is a tiny United Church and hall at the top of the hill above my house. Occasionally I go to the church to find that there are only about eight in the choir, and sometimes fewer than that in the pews. Through the week you can see cars gathered in the yards of those who have lived here for more than twenty years. It is the local card party rotating from house to house. Once in a while someone calls me to make sandwiches for it even though I have never been to one. Though I am on the edge of town, so close that I can walk in for a beer in forty minutes, I still live in the country. My mail still comes rural delivery and I cross the road to pick it up at about 9:30 each weekday morning. It is a ritual that I look forward to.

When I leave this place I yearn for it. I miss the yard, the woodpile, the comfort of knowing just where I am. Sometimes I visit friends' houses with big great rooms and gas fires and long clean countertops, and feel either envious of their place and wish to change mine to be more like it, or alternatively as if there is something wrong with me for not wanting more. I come home feeling unsatisfied, irritated by the creaky corners, the dust, and the single bathroom. Yet, this house, on this piece of land, is what I chose, and though sometimes I wonder if it's right, most times I know it is. Regardless, I tell myself it is what I have. There are times I yearn for more but I try to quell it, remembering the words I read somewhere: "Enough is an abundance." Like many people around me I struggle with wanting more and not appreciating what I have. Pretty things abound, and I reach for them like a crow reaches for a ruby. When I am alone in the house, though, and I come up the stairs to my little studio, I feel as if I have everything I need. My hook, my wool, my books and papers, feed me and satisfy me. They are part of what I need from this place that edges its way into the country as you leave Amherst and head to Oxford, and when I am alone with them, the thought that they are not enough never crosses my mind.

Ask yourself what about that place is home before you start designing and hooking, and mull that over for a while.

Wanting What I Have

I am so small
on seven acres
beneath a starry sky
rich blues lit up by fireflies
in knee high grass surprising me with their light.

My pick-up sits in the front drive
beyond a grey shingled barn
housing mounds of colour
and freezing out the moths.

The pitch of my roof is perfect,
the green clapboard washed out
and smoke rising,
as I return from the woods
I see it all like it was someone else's.

March 2004

"Diamonds in the Sky" is
owned by my neighbour
Rosemary who never chases
them herself and sees the
value in what she has.

"Two Peaks on the Bay" is a play on the beauty of lime meeting royal blue.

Hooking the House

Most people begin designing rugs by first hooking their homestead, the home of their heart, the place that is most important to them. For many people this is the house they live in, their cottage, or the home they grew up in. It is the place that they feel they most belong to. Over the years I have helped countless people design and create this rug for themselves or as a gift for family members. Oftentimes when people design these types of rugs they make the mistake of trying to crowd in too many elements. It is important to get down to the essence of what matters, and decide what are the most important things that you want to show in the rug you are making. In a very large rug, there may be more room, but remember that the more elements you have, the harder it may be to define what is really important about the rug. I remember once working with a woman who wanted to add her husband's boat, car, dog, and a long list of other things to a mat she was making for him of their family cottage. As she kept adding things, the rug kept getting watered down, making it a smorgasbord. Finally I said to her, "What is the essence of the rug that you want to make for your husband?" When she thought about it, it was the cottage and the water, so we focused on that. Rugs with lots of tiny elements can be great folk art, but you need to decide what it is you want to convey. Sometimes a homestead can be about the corner of the house and the huge one-hundred-year-old lilac bush that grows beside it. The house itself might not even be the main focus. Ask yourself what about that place is home before you start designing and hooking, and mull that over for a while. You might even want to jot a few things down in your journal, or make a few sketches in your sketchbook.

The second decision is always truth or beauty. When I make rugs I almost always choose beauty over truth because I believe I am making art, and I most want to make it beautiful. It is a choice with no right or wrong, but you will likely have to face it, and because you are working with wool, you may have to make some compromises. These compromises are not so awful, really. They are part of making art. Many of the rugs shown in this chapter are dreamscapes that might be inspired by real places but are really just created in my head. If you want an image that reflects your homestead perfectly, taking a picture and having it enlarged to hang on your wall works well every time, and will reflect the place as it actually is. When you decide to make a rug of a place, you have decided to use your hook to create an idea and a feeling about a place that is important to you. You are not creating a replica but an impression. That is all it will ever be. It will remind you of the way you felt there, the smells that lingered there, and the people who brought that place to life for you. It is a sentimental journey, and the thoughts and stories that come to your mind as you hook a rug such as this will be as important as the final rug that hangs on your wall. Treat the making of it as a journey back in time, and enjoy the ride.

Sometimes a homestead can be about the corner of the house and the huge one-hundred-year-old lilac bush that grows beside it.

The Main Elements of Hooking Houses

When I hook a house I look at it as if I were painting or renovating a real house in a real community. I look at the colour I'd like to have the trim, the main colour of the house, the colour and texture of the roof shingles, and what is being reflected in the windows.

The trim and body colours of the house have to be chosen together. I like to lay both colours down upon the house, imagining the finished image. I tend to choose bright colours for the trim, so that it stands out. If the house is large and is a central and important part of the rug I will hook the trim with two or three rows of hooking. Often I will hook it a little more tightly around corners and eaves so that these details stand out more. The trim colour can be enhanced with a second trim colour, even a third, especially if you want your house to have a painted lady or Victorian architectural feel to it. I will often highlight the tops of windows with this extra colour, or the window bars. The trim should be a colour that is distinct from the body colour of the house if you want the lines of the house to be well defined. If you want a more subtle-looking place, then choose a colour that is closer to the body colour. In the rug with the paisley sky (page 33), each house has its own personality because it was "painted" in its own fashion.

One of the puzzles for me is hooking houses that are all one colour. For example, many houses are totally white. I use a pale grey, a pale yellow, or an off white to distinguish the trim of the house from the main part of the house. To distinguish a corner or an eave, I will sometimes use a thin line of black or dark grey, cut in number 4. (Machine-cut wool is numbered from 3 to 10 according to the width, with 3 being the narrowest.)

Hooking the trim is the most important element of hooking the house because it forms the lines of the house and defines its shape. If you want a wonky house, with wild lines and tilted roofs, you define that when you hook the trim. It is the bones of the house, the feature that defines the shape, giving it its lines and style, so start a

"Waves Rising." Rugs that feature houses can be embellished with fanciful borders and playful skies.

house by hooking the trim. Often I will use white or yellow as the trim colour because they are both strong and clear.

In a very large house you might want to accentuate the effect of clapboard or shingles by outlining this element when hooking the body of the house. I generally do not. I will often hook a clapboard house in straight lines across the house to approximate the look of wood siding. Often once I have the house trim clearly established I just fill in the body colour. This is the easiest part of the hooking. Once it has been well outlined you just fill it in.

The roof of the house is often a very large area, so it is necessary to pick a wool that will work well not only on the house but with the rest of your mat. So often a roof is hooked in black or navy, and then laid upon a background of dark green hills so the roof gets lost in the background, and the house becomes ill defined. Choose a

My brother-in-law Jim Murdoch rebuilt the trim around our front door, adding all the important Georgian details.

roof colour that matches the main body colour of the house. I like wools that have a little tweed, or a dark wool that has flecks of another colour. I will use plaids or nubbly textured wools as well because they give the look of asphalt shingles. Roofs can be accentuated with dormer windows, chimneys, or ladders. Occasionally I have even hooked a couple of sunbathers on low shed roofs as I remember young women lying out on the tarred roofs of our neighbours' sheds when I was growing up. A roof should not be dismissed as a black mass on top of the house. It is part of the architecture and design of the house and the effort you put into choosing the right colour will be worth it.

The inside of the windows is another important element because it is a detail, and it is in the details that we get to add story and beauty to our hooked mats. Often I will hook a person in the window looking out at the community. If there is a night sky in the rug I will fill the insides of one or all of the windows with varying shades of warm yellow to show that there is both life and light in the house. You can fill in the windows with a grey tweed to show the effect of glass, but pick a pretty grey tweed, one with flecks of pastel colours so that it shows that something is being reflected in the windows from the outside, or that you can see through the windows to the inside. The windows reflect the life that is going on in the house so you do not want to deaden the house with a heavy dark colour, unless you want to show it as abandoned. I look for fantastic and interesting yarns such as sari silk so I can add a spark to my houses through the windows.

"From Sea to Sky." Though the houses are the focal point of this rug, they are embellished with fancy fish and dancing paisleys.

The door may be a tiny element of the house, but if you believe all the home-design shows, the colour of the door can affect how a person feels about a house, even whether or not they will buy it. One of my friends, Krista, who loves her house, likes to change the colour of her front door every spring. As the sun warms the early evening and I begin my spring walks in her neighbourhood, I see her coming out with paint chips in hand. What will it be this year? I wonder. For the price of a can of paint she gets to change the look and feel of her entryway, freshening things up, and pleasing herself every time she walks in the door. The colour of the door on your rug matters too. If it is too close to the trim colour, it will blend into the trim and look like a blob. It should be at least a shade or two darker or lighter than the trim colour, or in contrast to the trim colour. Either will work. It should also complement or contrast with the main body colour of the house. If the door is large you might want to add some detail by adding to or outlining its architectural features.

TIPS FOR HOOKING THE MAT

1. Put your pattern onto an embroidery frame or quilting hoop. It should lie flat and be tight like a drum. As you hook, keep your burlap tight on your frame as this makes the hooking quite a bit easier.

2. Your wool should be clean and ready to use. You can cut it into one-quarter- to one-half-inch strips. A simple method for cutting wool is to take an eight-by-four-inch rectangle of wool cloth, fold it accordion-style, and cut it into strips. This saves a lot of time and works best with five-and-a-half-inch scissors as they have a shorter blade.

3. Take a strip of wool and hold it underneath your pattern. Take your hook, holding it in your hand as you would a pencil. Put the hook through a hole in the burlap, wrap the wool around the hook on the underside of the burlap, and pull the end of the wool up through the hole. Continue doing this with the same strip of wool, pulling it up loop by loop to the top side of your pattern.

4. It is a good idea to start by outlining something near the centre of your pattern.

5. Continue to hook in every second or third hole, depending on the width and thickness of your wool. When your strip is used up, pull the end of the strip to the top side of your pattern, and clip the end so that it is an even height with your loops. Your loops should be one-quarter to one-third of an inch in height.

There are wools to covet when hooking houses. I like to have a hoard of clear bright solids for trims, doors, and main colours. I think these elements need to be in solid colours most of the time. Though if a house is stone or brick, you might be happy to use a nice woolly tweed, as it will give a natural effect. I also like a good selection of dark plaids, red plaids, chocolates, and deep greys with flecks of colour in them. I save small scraps of pretty multicoloured yarns to highlight the insides of windows.

6. You can hook in straight or curved lines. Be careful not to cross the paths of your wool on the back of the pattern. Always clip your wool and start in a new place, rather than carrying a colour across the back of your mat, otherwise your rug will be bulky, messy, and easy to pull out.

7. Continue to hook, outlining and filling in all the areas of your rug. Do not hook too tightly or your mat will not lie flat. It is the packing of the loops together that keeps the loops from falling out, but if you pack it too tightly your rug will curl up.

8. There are many ways of finishing the edges of a rug. You can sew by hand black cotton twill tape around the outside edges of the rug. Hook right up to the twill tape, or sew it on after the rug is hooked. When your rug is complete, you can roll two inches of the excess burlap into the twill tape and hand sew it along the backside of your rug. If the rug is going on the wall, you can fold the excess burlap along the back side of the rug, and sew it up. I like to press the rug with a hot iron and a wet cloth. This is called "blocking" the rug and it helps give it a finished patina and even out the loops.

9. When you hook, try not to go from left to right but cover many parts of the rug's area in case you should run short of wool. If you do this you can always add more wool of a slightly different colour to complete your rug. It may even enhance the primitive quality of your design.

10. Hooking rugs is meant to be a pleasant pastime. To avoid getting sore shoulders or hands, take lots of breaks, and make sure you are sitting in a comfortable position and that your body is relaxed. If you are comfortable, relaxed, and have support for your back, the hooking will go along much more easily.

Detail of a textured field rug. My field rugs emerged from walking the same stretch of road every day and noticing the details on either side.

CHAPTER 3
Walking into the Landscape

Five Miles a Day

I walk the same stretch of road every day. My feet hit the pavement every morning, in all types of weather. Some days everything looks the same, other days, everything looks different, the difference being how I am feeling, my attitude, and my energy. I began walking when my son was a little boy, and my husband would come home for lunch. In that hour I would take ten minutes just to hear my own thoughts, to be independent of a child for a few minutes. It began as ten or fifteen minutes a day, as a chance to be alone. I found being a mother at home stifling, and the walking settled those feelings away for me. Walking was a retreat back to myself.

I quickly learned that the walking eased all the physical aches I had from sitting at my rug-hooking frame for long stretches at a time. A body that hooks rugs, for any long length of time, needs a little soothing. In about six months I had formed the habit of a twenty-minute walk every day. Slowly over time I increased it by walking a little further each day. In time I began walking in the morning before my husband left for work. Eventually my children went to school and I was free to walk as often as I liked. It has turned out that I walk twice a day for a total of an hour and a half. Through it all I never lost any weight but I dropped three sizes in my jeans and

"November." This field rug is more abstract than many, and the grey sky and rose-tinted landscape lead to thoughts of winter.

my legs when I straighten them are as hard as rocks. I feel better generally, and I rarely have any lower back or shoulder aches from leaning into my rug frame.

It still amazes me that walking has made me nicer. Yes, just plain nicer. I am not as grumpy, and when I am grumpy I often go for a walk. Perhaps I would have gotten kinder with age anyway but I believe the routine of walking has strengthened my character. Some people feel that age alone makes them kinder. Debbie Frenette, a friend of mine, told me that she really enjoyed her forties because she stopped letting stupid little things bother her. She said it was in her forties she came to understand life better, and learned that it was not all about what she was feeling and thinking. She might be right, but for me, I have to add walking to aging. It helps me sort out my thoughts and feelings. It gives me a chance to think through the day, and to rant without having to be heard. My rants seem to be less tyrannical most of the time. A lot of what I think and feel is best left to my walks. The motion of heel, to sole, to toe has made me stronger and kinder. I am harder in the body, and softer in the heart.

The winter is hard on walkers. In the rain or ice I sometimes walk at the Amherst Stadium. The community built an inside walking track and it is well used. The track, with its cushy blue flooring, is a narrow lane that circles above the ice surface. As I walk I can see the delicate little figure skaters, or the big rough old-timers hacking away at the puck, depending on the time of day. Last week I saw Creighton Marney, the local optometrist who prescribed my first pair of glasses to me twenty-five years ago, ahead of me in a navy-blue ski jacket. As I came up behind Creighton, I saw that he was hunched over at the shoulders, lost in thought. Gently I said hello as I passed him, and he smiled and said, "This gets rid of all my anger." Creighton is eighty-seven, and from all appearances does not seem angry about anything. I could not help but think…does this mean that I too will still be walking in forty-three years to stave off anger and frustration?

"Field and Fence Post." There is so much more colour in a field than we notice at first glance.

Sometimes I think of my walking as a way to fend off an inner madness that lurks under my skin. What did I used to do with this excess energy? I thought that those feelings settled with age, and that by the time I was Creighton's age I'd be walking just because, rather than to get rid of angry feelings that come sometimes from nowhere,

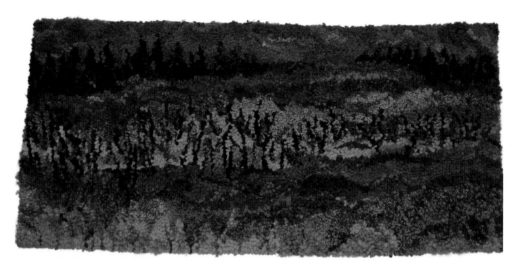

"On the edge of October." This rug was inspired by my morning walk, which ends at a field of alders.

and sometimes just from being a mother and a wife. I am wonderful and terrible at being a mother and a wife; it just depends on when you catch me. Creighton took me aback, because I often think of my feelings as being situational, and he reminded me that they are not. My feelings come from being who I am. Sometimes I am crotchety and angry when I am alone and haven't seen anyone for hours, and that is just because I'm me, not because of any responsibilities I have. Walking has helped me understand that, and take responsibility for myself and my moods.

I will probably always have to walk to deal with minor anxieties, and general contrariness. Our friend Walter Oake says to Robert, my husband, "She can't help it. Newfoundlanders are crooked." Being from a Newfoundland background himself, he knows that the idea of Newfoundlanders as perfectly pleasant is a myth. Live with them, they are just like anyone else, and according to plenty of us, naturally crabby souls, at least in their own houses. My eleven-year-old daughter says I have "meanypants" and "snappypants." I tell her I also have "happy pants" and she says, "Why don't you put them on?" The beauty of her being eleven is that she doesn't yet know

"The grapevine and field." I love using fleece and interesting yarns freely in a mat. It is so liberating to pick and choose from a big pile of textured wools laid on my frame.

that as she grows up she'll be fitting into her mother's pants quite well. My general feelings of contrariness, according to Creighton Marney, will last a lifetime, and the walking will continue to serve as a tonic. So walking is good for my mind, as well as my body, but the softening of my heart has been the real virtue of my daily treks.

My walks also generate ideas. Sometimes I get a nice sentence that could start a little story. Sometimes I imagine a rug. These things don't happen when I first start out; they are the markers of the halfway point when I have stopped ranting and thinking about myself and allowed myself to just be mindful or "relax" or "think."

My ideas have been allowed to simmer and sometimes they bubble up and insist upon being heard. Whether or not they get acted upon is another story altogether.

My field rugs emerged from walking, and I think they are among some of the best rugs I have made. One day on a walk I saw a white farmhouse peeking out above a field that was green on first glance, and awash with colour on second glance. All of a sudden I saw the side of the road like I had never seen it before. It was as if I had woken up from a ten-year sleep and rugs like "The grapevine and field" (page 51) started happening. Walking the same stretch of road time and time again can be demanding on the imagination. At first it is hard to see it differently. Even the cars that drive by contain the same people. My imagination began to demand that I look at the little things. I began to see the creatures, the depth of the grass, the colour of the leaves, the way the light falls on the trees. I began to wait for the pileated woodpeckers that nest somewhere above the pumping station. Now I count the crows, and watch for the iridescence on their wings. I listen for the mourning doves because their solemn cry reminds me of sadnesses gone by. I keep my eye out for the beavers by the dam, and remember the time one of them ran across the road in front of me, slapping its tail against the pavement, mad that I was out so early on a summer morning.

My walk has become about keeping an eye out for the albino deer that stalks the neighbourhood, and saying a prayer that no hunter will have the heart to shoot it. The rosehips, I notice, are ever changing, as are the old abandoned orchards. In spring they are young and crisp and fresh. In summer they are lush and hidden by a bevy of leaves. In fall they start to show their wear but bear fruit, and in the winter they become brittle, and their fruit hangs on by a thread waiting for a harsh wind to blow, or a bird to find it.

Light changes the landscape here within a moment, transforming fresh crisp mornings to solemn shadowy days. When I started to look closely, I discovered that I could not anticipate what I would see from one second to the next. The predictability is willingly

"In my yard." The sky with its tiny paisleys makes this field rug more playful than serious, as do the casts of mauve throughout it.

forsaken for beauty, and the relationship endures because I am in love with the light. I look at the sky for signs but am only taken in by the largesse and majesty of it. The other night as I looked up at the sky above my yard, it was full of swooping purple swirls. I felt as if I had never been in this spot before. I saw that I am so small, and the world is so big, and this I have learned on a road full of scrub and brush with a creek that dries up in summer and a river that is so small few know it is there. Right under my foot one day there is a purple salamander with orange spots, like a small child's rubber toy. On another I find a perfectly preserved dragonfly with its blue-black lace wings and striped back. A summer's preserves at my feet. Other days there are small birds lying dead like a sketch from a botany book. All these things matter because I am there.

Once after I read a passage from Alice Walker's book *The Color*

"Fish Houses on the Coast." This rug played with aqua against the green hills. It now offers inspiration and acts as a buffer on the walls of a sound studio.

Purple about Celie's relationship with God and her feeling that God was everywhere in nature, I was left a little bewildered. The next morning on my walk, by the side of the road I saw a deer that had been hit. I immediately understood that if I cut a tree my arm would bleed too, just like Celie's. All of a sudden I understood. That is what happens on a walk, when you listen to the sounds in the woods, and to your heart, and to your own mind; you hear these things and you come to understandings. Lights come on. You hear so much, yet somehow through all that noise, your mind becomes quieter. You learn to be quiet with it.

I have seen that a season changes a twenty-acre field, like twenty years change a woman. The land is so different from season to season that it is unrecognizable. It even changes within the season, though these changes are sometimes more subtle. A green field in the summer is really a profusion of colour when you walk along it, and you see that the shades in it change daily as one flower blooms and another fades. Walking the same stretch of road has forced me to notice the little things. It has stretched my mind, and made it a container for all kinds of wonderful details that I once ignored. I rely on it like a plant relies on water, and when I get it I am all the better for it. It has changed my rugs profoundly because it has opened my eyes to the natural world and let me into a room in my own mind that is full of surprises.

Hooking the Landscape

A routine can help you see the beauty in the smallest of things. In his book *Beauty* John O'Donohue, the Irish poet and philosopher, spoke about how light paints the landscape. He explained that though we see the same landscape day after day, the light is like an artist transforming it so that we never actually get to see it the same way twice.

On a boat ride you really get the feeling of being under a big sky. There you are on the ocean, like in the famous Breton fisherman's prayer, and you become aware that your boat is so small, and the ocean is so big. After a ferry ride across Placentia Bay I arrived back at a friend's house all excited about how blue the ocean was. I was mesmerized by the colour of the cliffs. The first thing she said in response was, "What colour was the sky?" She understood that the light had been painting the landscape, and she wanted me to remember that. The sky was bright blue, and thus the ocean was more blue than usual. Had the sky been grey, had the time of day been different, the landscape would have transformed itself.

Understanding the transformative power of light is helpful but not necessary for hooking excellent rugs. You do not even have to walk every day but you do need to be a student of the landscape you want to recreate, walking through it and noticing the light, because it allows you to look at the landscape closely, and admire it. When you walk away from it, close your eyes and try to recreate it in your mind. Remember the colours, the lines, the shapes of the trees, the texture of the field. Whatever happens in the studio happens because you have been paying attention and living your life. So the first and most important step to creating great landscape rugs is to study the

"Barns behind the field." I love blue, the colour of forget-me-nots or delphiniums in a field. It is so warm and speaks of summer.

world around you, drinking up the colours and taking in the texture of the fields, hills, and craggy rocks. Working from a picture is one thing, but getting to know the land with your own two eyes will lend a new dimension to what you can offer to your rugs.

When you actually get ready to sit down to make the mat you should already have your inspiration in mind. There is no good design without inspiration. By the time you sit down to design the mat, you will have sketched it out and played with your ideas a little. Before you put the hook to the frame you will understand and know the character of the landscape you are trying to capture. There are many simple techniques that can help you create sweeping landscapes that romance the eye and are interesting to look at.

The first thing you must decide is the subject of the landscape. Just what type of landscape do you want to create? Once you choose the subject or place you want to recreate in a mat you will have to decide on the important elements that need to be included. Pare it down to those elements that give you the feeling of the place. For example, in a large, rambling farm-scape you might choose to put in the house, the two barns, the big elm tree, and the rose bushes. You might decide to leave out the battered chicken coop and the broken-down truck, depending of course on the feeling you want to create. You might decide just to have a corner of the house off in the distance. One place can be captured in hundreds of different ways. How do you see it? If you want a quiet, pastoral feeling, perhaps the truck and coop are out. If you want a lonesome feeling you might want to leave in some of the rundown elements. You can also feel free to change things around, omitting power lines, or adding in a flower garden. Remember you want to create a beautiful mat and this may require a little adapting. The other important thing to remember is that a subject is not finite. Remember to edit. Know what to leave out. Get rid of the objects that obscure the view, crowd it, or throw off the composition. It is as simple as this: no one ever adds in the garbage box at the end of the rural lane. It just might not belong in the artwork, even though it may belong in real life.

Whatever happens in the studio happens because you have been paying attention and living your life.

The same landscape can be captured over and over again, in different lights, and by changing the elements of the picture. Think of how the Group of Seven painters went back to the same kinds of landscapes again and again. They were in love with those landscapes. Think of Emily Carr's relationship with the British Columbia forest. It captivated her. Often artists are discouraged from looking at the same subject too closely. It is thought that they are not moving forward. I like to think that sometimes I am on a slow train ride in my work, and that gives me a chance to look at one area really closely. You can create a series or use a particular landscape as a theme in your work. This allows you to focus on different details and different feelings each time you approach it. It gets rid of the feeling that you have to do it exactly right the first time, and can loosen you up a little. Subjects do not end because you hook them once. You can approach a landscape again and again, trying to emphasize different elements of it.

I love to play with the same subject matter over and over again. I will often hook a landscape in different formats. You can sketch it as a close-up, a panoramic view, a horizontal view, a vertical, or a wide-open view. Play with the shape of your rugs. Think of squares, circles, oddly shaped edges, as possible formats for a landscape. In a close-up you might pick out a house or a tree and really focus in on the details. The panoramic view shows a long narrow slice of the landscape, allowing you to create sweeping fields and show a broad landscape. It is one of my favourite formats because so many different elements of the landscape can be shown in a single mat. A tall, thin mat allows you to show distance well as you can layer fields and hills and houses, showing elements of the landscape that might be miles away. A wide-open format is usually a fat rectangle and allows you to show some expanse and some depth. It is a very traditional format and works well for many subjects. You can also create a series of rugs in the form of a diptych or triptych. I like to create series of squares of related landscapes that are not all necessarily a part of one larger image but separate images created in the same format.

The way that you see the landscape you want to re-create will often determine the format, but you might have to play around with it to decide. You will have a natural instinct towards a certain shape or format. Know though that you have some choice here, and can expand the horizon, if you like. The sketching of the landscape in different formats will get you thinking about your subject more clearly, and help you know it better. It will make you consider the land, and that will be time well spent.

Traditionally in landscapes there are three areas to consider: no matter which format you choose, you will divide that format into the foreground, the middle ground, and the background. The foreground is the lead-in to your landscape. In this area I often put a point of interest to draw the viewer into the mat, such as a bit of a fence and a bunch of bushes, or even the edge of a building. The middle ground is often the main part of the mat and holds many of the important elements of the subject. The background is the furthest away from

"Apple Blossom Spring." There is a free use of rose fleece here, hooked with abandon.

the front of the mat and is the part that leads you to the sky. These are the main parts of traditional landscape composition. In creating a good composition for our rugs we are struggling to create the very best arrangement of all the important elements of the landscape. You will need to carefully consider balance as you place these elements. You want the rug to have balance between the elements, as well as between the colours and textures you have chosen.

Once you have the design created or have chosen a landscape pattern, you may be left wondering how to get the wool to look like hills and fields. Well, if your hands are nimble and the wool cupboard is well stocked you can turn your wool cloth, yarn, and fleece into picturesque landscapes. These mats are all about texture. You want to take on texture, and begin to feel natural and comfortable working with it. In rugs, Sylvia MacDonald, a well-known Nova Scotia rug-hooking teacher, would say, "You are painting with wool."

If you want to hook great landscapes you will have to get used to using textures like the ones in the field rugs in this chapter. Textured wools allow you to add dimension to the landscape. Your stash of wool should include Shetland sweaters, angora sweaters, fancy yarns, mohair, natural sheep's wool dyed and undyed, thready fabrics, boucles, carded sheep's wool, tweeds and plaids, silk yarns, eyelash yarns, merino wool, wool jersey. You might also explore other bins at the secondhand store and see what kind of interesting fabrics there are to work with. Be fearless. As long as you enjoy hooking with it, it is worth playing with. There is nothing better than finding a great angora sweater or a green jersey dress for your wool cupboard, but trying new and other interesting fabrics could lead you to something even better. You will need a wide variety of shades, particularly of greens, golds, and blues. I also like rusts and ambers, wines, teals, and mauves in my field rugs. The colours you will need depend on the season you are depicting. It would be great if you could send someone out with a list of what you need, but it does not work like that. A great stash of wool is a work in progress and you need to keep picking up those fancy bits and pieces to keep your cupboard interesting and inspirational. It is the gathering together of many types of wool from many different places that makes our work charming. It is the old metaphor of weaving together the different bits of a life: a scarf from here, a ball of yarn you picked

TIPS FOR CHOOSING COLOUR

You can use the colours suggested for a project, or you can experiment by pulling in your favourite shades.

Do not be afraid to change the sky to a night sky or make the background darker or lighter. Colour is a personal statement. Put your stamp on the rug you are making.

Pull out the wools you have and lay them together on the mat, experimenting with what looks good. Quickly pull away the pieces that do not work.

A simple tip for creating a colour scheme is to find a plaid or tweed that you like and use it as the basis for your scheme by pulling the solid colours out and using these as the colour plan for your rug.

"Golden Field." The gold and amber hills tell us the time of year. Summer is gone, but winter is still a ways off.

up somewhere, that old coat of your sister's. Selection of texture and colour is essential. You will discover that there are as many colours in nature as one can imagine and that a large selection of both colour and texture is important. Remember that exactly the same colour in three different textures will act like three different wools in your mat. I love to use yellow cloth, yellow silk, and perhaps yellow merino yarn as if they were one colour for an area of a field because

Remember that if a colour does not work, you can always unhook it and use a different colour. Having said that, try not to keep hooking and rehooking.

If you cannot seem to get the right colour, go to another area of the rug and hook it. Sometimes focusing on another area of the mat will lead to the problem area working itself out.

You can create a shaded effect by mixing two or three colours that are close together and hooking them randomly in an area.

"Moon over a County Road" is inspired by the local blueberry fields as they turn red, and, of course, the moon when we see it in the daytime.

it gives dimension to the work, making the field feel like it has some movement, similar to the field in "Golden Field" (page 61).

I like to have three or four colours that are close together and can be used together in an area as if they were one kind of wool. This allows you to show light falling on the land. When I hook these landscapes or field rugs I like to hook large areas in one tone of the same colour. I lay out large areas of coloured wool cut up for easy access. It is tempting to keep changing colours every two or three strips but this would be a big mistake. It might give a confetti or hit-and-miss look to your rug, which will detract from the landscape. You do not want your rug to be spotty. A quick colour change is what is needed for close-ups and small details, but you want large areas of colour to show large expanses of land. You could use a dark line of a contrasting colour to separate one field from another, but it is not essential. One field can be separated from another just by contrasting the colours. For example you might have gold up against khaki green, and you'll clearly be able to see that there is a transition in this area of the mat, like the clear transitions in "Moon over a County Road."

When I hook the fields I try to hook in a directional way. If I want to show that the wind is blowing I will hook with a slant in the direction of the wind. If the pasture is a big rounded hill I will hook in big rounded strokes. I have spent many hours over the years studying landscape painting to see what I can learn from the painters' strokes. There is much to be learned and the ideas of oil painters can easily be translated to rug hooking. I encourage you to pore over the books of your favourite paintings or stand before them in galleries and study the way the painter has moved the paintbrush to get a desired effect.

The elements of the landscape can be almost anything, but typically they include sky, sea, rivers, ponds, trees, plants, bushes, grass, flowers, fences, and buildings. Other elements are often included depending on the area you are recreating. When I hook the sky I first think about what kind of day it is. I also consider what time of day it is. If it is a bright sunny day I need one set of blues. If it is the evening light I need a whole other set of colours, perhaps some grey blues and mauves. If a storm is approaching I need to get out some greys. For a bright day I like to gather several light baby blues together and some natural sheep's wool for clouds. I hook the clouds first and add in the blues afterward. I like to hook each of the blues in large fat areas like cumulus clouds themselves, working it up really close to the clouds of sheep's wool. This gives the effect of a large sunny day. If evening was approaching I would add some mauves, or even the palest yellow to the mix. I might also hook the lower parts of the sky in long thinner areas rather than big cumulus areas. Sky contributes a lot to the overall feeling of the rug, and the colours you choose for it should relate to the rest of the colours you use in the landscape. Remember there is a relationship between sea, sky, and land. The colours of all of these are affected by each other.

The sea is dependent on the same things as the sky. A stormy sea might require aquas, deep blues, navy, and some deep blue-greens.

"Joggins." This is the view from my friend Edna Boone's window in Joggins, NS. It's one of the finest beaches I've walked.

A calm sea might need up to four shades of nearly exactly the same deep blue. Tidal water might need to be a brown over dyed blue so that you can see the mud rising underneath the water. Pendleton shirts, with their dark blue and aqua plaids, make great water, but I always add a few different wools for interest. I do not like to hook a plaid as the only wool for any important element of the landscape because it looks as if that is just what I did. I like to mix it up and make it interesting, drawing the viewer in to see just what is going on after they have first been captivated by the overall image.

Natural sheep's wool makes plants and trees come off the mat so that they become a point of interest. For trees, bushes, and plants I like to show the branches with a bit of dark brown, or a deep wine. For the leaves I will often hook dyed green sheep's wool very high to show a puffiness. When I use sheep's wool I often hook it high, up to an inch, then when I take the next loop it pulls it back down again. Also using sheep's wool, I take a puffy piece and sort of hand-card it into a loose strand and hook it gently. The thinner and looser the strand, the further it will go. If it has a nice curly end I will sometimes leave that end up, and not trim it off, so that it has a dramatic windblown effect.

Multicoloured and variegated yarns become an instant flower garden when hooked and accentuated with a bit of green. Flowers and flower gardens are also easy to recreate with dyed sheep's wool and fancy yarns hooked up with a little green beside them. Take several colours of sheep's wool and keep changing the colour, hooking a small area of one colour and poking a little green in beside it. I like to hook the sheep's wool in colourful squiggly vertical lines as these approximate tall standing flowers like hollyhocks, delphinium, or liatris. Think of the shapes of the flowers you want to approximate and try to give the impression of their shape with the wool. Once you step back from it, your little mess will transform itself from a few bits of woolies to grandma's garden back at the homestead. I did a one-

"September." In this rug the red field adds a stark contrast to the lime and blue.

day workshop on using these wools in this way, and it was amazing what people came up with in their gardens. Some added a little grey tweed and formed rock gardens. Others hooked in tiny bits of silk ribbon, almost as flecks, and showed delicate low ground covers. The more you experiment, the more you will learn. Remember that flowers will create a point of interest, and you should distribute the colour in a way that works for the overall mat. Think about where you add these dramatic flourishes as they have a lot of impact.

In very primitive design, a building is squared off at the bottom. These field rugs are more impressionistic. When you hook a building you can give it a feeling of being in the distance by bringing the land up to meet it rather than squaring off the bottom. Avoid using textured wools in the buildings as this will confuse them with the landscape. Let them recede into the landscape by using plain woollens in solid colours. I generally look for subtle colours in the houses in these rugs because though I sometimes want to use a building as a point of interest or to show some life, I do not want it to be the focal point of the rug. I want people to be carried over that field like they are on a magic carpet. Often in my field rugs the house will be cream or grey, so that it stands out from the landscape but does not overpower it.

When you are hooking landscapes you must remember that your stash of wool needs to be interesting and exciting if your rug is going to be these things. You must be a student of the landscape you want to create. Know it and watch it and this will come through in your rugs. Finally, all good landscapes follow some basic design principles that are centred around composition, balance, and format. Do not be afraid to experiment. These rugs require texture as it adds the dimension they need. Hook in broad sweeping areas, thinking about the shape of the area you are hooking as an acre or two of land. I use nice curved lines for hills, contrasting this when I create spruce trees with small dashes of dark colours hooked across in zigzag fashion. The direction that you hook in will be seen in the finished rug and is part of the beauty. As you hook landscapes, relax your hands and mind as if you were going for a gentle walk on the land itself, and your rug will tell the tale of your journey.

The vet up the road from me used to farm a few fields on the way

WORKING WITH TEXTURE IN HOOKED RUGS

Interesting yarns and cloths can take a rug from a flat plane to a sculptural textile, making its beholder want to reach out and touch it, to feel the quality of the cloth in it. Somehow adding texture to a rug makes it seem more real, more picturesque. Hooking with texture is the same as hooking with regular wool cloth or yarn. I like to take the natural sheep's wool and pull it gently into a five- or six-inch strip, then hook it the same as I would a piece of cut cloth. I do tend to pull it higher. I also let the loops stand out from the rest of the rug. Some highly textured wool cloths or sweaters may need to be hand-cut into strips rather than using a cutter.

If you are using fine yarns or very thin fibres, it is a good idea to strand them together to hook if you want those fibres to be more pronounced. For a more subdued look, try hooking the fibre as a single strand. This will give you a fine texture. For landscape you can use almost any fabric, in nearly any shade. Golds, rusts, and other autumn shades will give the earth a mellow, somewhat parched appearance. Bright yellows, reds, and purples will stand out as flowers. Greens will give dimension to the land or to town. One year he filled it with a mauve timothy that blew in the wind. Another year it was filled with sunflowers. These fields became big and beautiful mounds of colour. There seemed to be more beauty than one field could possibly hold. When I drive around the countryside I sometimes think if I were a farmer I would plant a field of yellow here, or wheat here. With my field rugs I get to take three acres, fill it with mauve phlox, then surround it with wheat fields, and plant a bunch of lupines in that far corner. It makes me feel as if I am a grand gardener, with a master plan. Really, when I do this, I am no different from an eleven-year-old playing with Lego. I am in an imaginary world, absorbed completely, and when I come out, I feel so thankful that I am still able to get to my own personal Narnia.

bushes. I like to use multicoloured slub because the variegated quality changes the look of the land.

The more you work with different varieties of material, the greater understanding you will have of what they can do for you. You will need to experiment with texture to understand it better and gain greater control over how you can make it work for you. Try it, even if you think it might not be quite right. Do not be afraid to use something unusual; do not prejudge what can and cannot be used. Push your limits and occasionally override what you think is your better judgement—that is how you learn to work more competently with fibre, and how you put your own creative stamp on your work. Rug hooking is forgiving; you can always pull it out if it is not working and try another colour, texture, or fabric.

Some people also find that they like to use different hooks for different textures. You may find that you will use one hook for cut cloth and another altogether for wool roving.

"Mermaidens." There is nothing more magical than the idea of mermaids.

CHAPTER 4
Magic and Storytelling

The Marvellous is All Around Us

My mother's death seems so long ago now, but I'll never forget the magic that seemed to float about me that day. I had small children, both under nine. I had that tired stance that mothers take, before they know that it only gets worse as the children get to be teenagers and become even more demanding. Regardless, I thought I was worn down and tired, so I planned to take a full day to myself in early April and head to the Northrop Frye Literary Festival in Moncton, New Brunswick. I got up on a beautiful spring morning and drove myself to Moncton, where I spent the morning wandering through a huge bookstore looking at art books. I came across a big thick book of paintings of nudes by Lucien Freud. I spent an hour with that book. I have never been formally educated as an artist and this was the first time I had seen his paintings. I was captivated by the book; it was full of images of large, bulky nude women in slightly askew poses. They were a little dark but deeply compelling. There were everyday-looking women, slightly overweight, bony, bulging, all types of bodies painted nude. They looked alone and solitary, but uncompromised. I knew that they were exquisite. I wanted to buy the book, but it was $150. I had never paid such a price for a book, and I reluctantly left it behind. I could not imagine that a book could cost so much. I settled instead for a $29 book of Mary Cassatts, with very beautiful but very sentimental paintings of mothers and daughters. I still have it, but every time I visit a bookstore I look for that Lucien Freud book. No doubt I should have bought it.

I then took myself out to lunch at a fromagerie. Moncton has a strong Acadian culture. The influence of the many French artists in the area gives it a great creative flavour that I was enjoying. I sat with a notebook over tea for an hour or so before heading to a festival workshop with Robert Bly on writing poetry. It was the first time I had ever been to a writing workshop, and I was not really familiar with Bly's poetry. I just wanted to go off by myself and learn something for the day. I hadn't written many poems, but I wanted to. I wanted to play with the idea of writing poetry. That day Bly asked us to write a poem about our parents. He demanded we not write about what they did wrong, but about something they did right. I liked him when he said this. I liked his "Stop the self pity, don't indulge, get on with your life" approach. It is so easy to reflect on the sadness in our past, so easy to slip into melancholy when you go to reflect or to write. He asked us to examine that as we approached a subject, and avoid it. I did not feel particularly inspired right away so I thought about the inspirations I used for my rugs, and the words that were behind them. I came to a rug about my mother, a portrait I had made, and I wrote a poem about that, about her teaching me to eat cod's head stew. I was pleased with the poem as I left the workshop and headed home at about three o'clock. I felt good about the sunshine, the warm April air. Even my green boucle sweater felt good over my black shirt and pants. It was spring and one of the first days we could shed our coats. Everything felt good. I felt like everything was fine.

When I got home an hour later there was no one home and my frame was sitting there waiting for me to hook. The pleasure of the solitude, the freedom to hook quietly without children running through the room, seemed to be a perfect ending to the day. I sat and hooked uninterrupted until about seven o'clock, when the staff from the home where my mother lived called to say she had taken sick. I got in the car and headed out there quickly. On the way I heard an ambulance but I headed to her place anyway. When I got there they

"Mother Watches Over" captures the perspective of a child, the way it must feel to have your mother watching you all the time.

told me she had been taken to the hospital by ambulance already. I could tell from the look on the nursing staff's face that my mother was gone. I knew it. I arrived at the hospital, and was brought to her. She lay there in a pale green room alone on a gurney, naked under a thin sheet. During her Friday night bath she had had a heart attack and died almost instantly. There she lay, like a painting from the Lucien Freud book that I had seen that morning, so beautiful and unencumbered. She all of a sudden looked like the woman I used to bathe with in our bright little yellow bathroom in Freshwater when I was seven. There was her hernia, her breasts, her strong muscular legs—all that had seemed so beautiful and so interesting to me as a child. She no longer looked like the small woman she had become with the strain of aging and illness, and there was no longer the sadness she felt about coming towards the end of her life. She looked strong, and I felt the strength of her spirit in the room. I felt like she was all around me. This all happened in the matter of seconds, of course, before the local doctor whooshed in and a nurse called my friend Nancy, another nurse, to come to the hospital until my sisters arrived. Understandably, others needed to be called, yet I felt so peaceful, and glad to have been there for those few seconds, alone with her in that room. I said a few prayers, ones that perhaps she herself had taught me.

"Man at the Table." This rug reminds me of many of the fathers on the hill where I grew up.

I was ready for her death, and being alone with her under those austere lights, surrounded by those pale walls, came as no surprise to me. My mother was seventy-eight, and she had a heart attack in her bath on a Friday night and died suddenly. Those paintings in the morning, that poetry writing in the afternoon, the rare time to myself, all got me ready for what was happening. When I looked back on the day I felt there had been some kind of magic on my path.

My father and I also shared a bit of magic. The last time I saw him conscious I was called to his nursing home on a Saturday night. He had been sick for years and had lain nearly dormant in a bed with dementia. I was frequently called in because he was sick, but this time he was just unsettled and the nurses called concerned. When I was a child my father and I would watch TV in his room at night as he rolled and smoked cigarettes. There would be white curls of smoke between us, and a black-and-white Philips TV before us. We would be alone there, with my mother gone to bingo. It was on those nights that my father would tell me how he always dreamed of writing a book but never could, and formed in me a desire to write my own. We were quietly happy together. He would sometimes carve away on a piece of pine, wood chips falling to the carpeted floor. It was the 1970s, before smoking was a curse and bingo was considered gambling. Up until the time I was about fourteen this was our routine.

The night I was called in to the home, we could not settle him so I said to the nurse that perhaps if we rolled him up to the TV room, we could turn the TV on and I could sit with him there until he fell asleep. He had slept with the TV on all night, every night of my childhood. It was the only thing I could think of. We brought him up near the nurses' desk, slid his bed into the quiet and abandoned chapel, and turned on the television. When I turned it on there were Emmylou Harris and Don Williams singing a duet, "Would You Come if I Needed You?" As a child, my mother would lie with me until I fell asleep, and every night at the same time the announcer on CJON radio would play a Don Williams song. I don't know if my father ever knew this or not—it does not matter. I am comforted by Don Williams. As for the lyrics, of course, how could they be any clearer? I would come if he needed me. It was just another tiny miracle, or another big coincidence, depending on your perspective. I choose to believe that life is a series of tiny miracles. I suppose some might think that makes me weak minded. I can't help it; life makes me weak sometimes, and I am overcome with the wonder of it all. May I always be so lucky. My father had the clearest, bluest eyes. They danced when he told one story, and filled with tears just as easily when he told another. That night he looked at me with those clear blue eyes and I told him the only thing I knew, that I loved him, and that it was okay for him to leave, that things would be okay. By the time the song was over, my father was peacefully asleep and he never woke after that. He did not die until a week later, and

> *My father had the clearest, bluest eyes. They danced when he told one story, and filled with tears just as easily when he told another.*

I almost did not believe my sister Donna when she called to say that he was going. She insisted that he was, so I went in. We had been called to my father's bed so many times over the years. The first time I remember I was just a youngster of four or five, and I was brought to see him through a glass partition for one reason or another. It was at the Placentia Cottage Hospital. For years I had been called to his bedside, and I was beginning to believe he would live forever. Thankfully Donna knew, and I was there when he did die. I felt his spirit slip away. I am sure I did. I think being at my father's side when he died was the closest I have ever gotten to feeling that God was a real presence in my life. At the death of both my parents I felt that spirit was more powerful than life, and what is that, if it is not God? Their spirits, of course, did not slip completely away. They remain around me, and now and again feel imminently present.

One of those times when I felt my father's presence was a few years ago when I was visiting Placentia with my friend Tish. We landed in St. John's and drove out around the bay right away. As soon as we got settled in we took a walk, up to the graveyard and down onto the beach. I stopped on the beach in Placentia on the big grey and mauve round rocks, looking across the water at my childhood home on Old Settlement Hill in Freshwater. Our white house was perched on a hill, and my view of it was perfect. When I looked down at my feet there was a small carved wooden boat. It was a little tan cape islander that had washed up on shore and laid itself at my feet, as a gift for me. I picked it up, and looked back at that very same house where as a child I had sat by my father as he carved ducks and boats and puffins from small blocks of pine and sold them to Nonia, the nurses' union gift shop in St. John's. I was stirred by the magic of it. It was as if he was there to welcome me home. Now, I know, of course, that my father did not carve this particular boat, but I do believe that there was a little mystery happening that day on the beach in Placentia, and that I felt the spirit of my father with me, on the rocks, with my little boat, looking across the water to my old home.

Mystery surrounds us. All the world is full of magic, though your spirit has to be somewhat open to receive it. Harry Thurston, a poet and family friend, once said that he is confounded by our "denial of the marvellous." The most magical, mystical things can happen to us and we feel the need to explain them away. Another friend, Donny Miller, a Baptist minister and a playwright, says, "Well, Deanne, if you can believe in God, you can believe in anything." Most people, when asked, still profess to believe in God, though they may not be religious or belong to a church. Yet

"Cape Islander Boat." This little boat is similar in style to the carved boat I found on the beach in Placentia.

few of us believe in miracles, and many of us are challenged when confronted with the magic in everyday life. We are quiet about it in a crowded room, but in truth, most of us have a story or a magical encounter that has left us wondering. I do not know what life is about, and I am left only to wonder about the mystery and the magic of it all, but I do know that these things exist. The power of our lives is in our stories and most of us have stories that are greater than ourselves. Most of us at one time or another have felt that we are a tiny part of something bigger, something more powerful than ourselves, a time when we realize that life itself is magic.

Putting a Little Magic into the Mat

Most times when I hook a rug I put a little spirit into it, and never worry whether it is ever seen or understood. I think of it as my own little secret in the mat. Flavouring your mat with a little magic

Detail from "Visiting on the way from Church." As these women leave they talk to each other about their stories.

is more about making it than it is about the finished product. Sometimes I will write words in the landscape or water that you can only make out after you have stared at the rug for a good long while. Sometimes I write a thought or an idea and hook right over it, so it is only written on the canvas, and never seen. You could write a love note on the burlap, when you are hooking it for someone you love, and just hook right over it so the only person who ever knows it to be there is you. It is about putting spirit into your mat. As you hook it, you can't help but reflect upon how you feel about that person. You are, after all, making the rug with love; why not tuck in a little secret? Silly, you think? Well, perhaps it is, but the whole notion of magic and spirit, even love sometimes, can come off as a little silly. But where would art be without any of these things? Soft as they are, they are the backbone of art, and art, I believe, is the backbone of our culture. Putting your spirit into the mat takes a little risk, a little fooling around, a dash of playfulness, and a need to forget yourself and all the things you are certain of. You have to let go a little bit, let thoughts and ideas flow, come and go easily as you sit to hook.

Sometimes when I make a special rug for someone I love I tuck in a special fabric, one that has meaning to me or the person who will receive it, and that adds a little bit of magic. Mostly, though, I hook in all the thoughts I have as I create the rug. When I give them the rug, I give them all the spirit, all the magic, and all that I experienced while I created it. That is the gift you give when you make someone a mat; it is your energy and commitment that they receive.

Remember in the beautiful story *Like Water for Chocolate* how the tears the woman cried as she made the food led the people who ate it to cry, and when she cooked with joy, they ate with joy? Our mats are our art, they are our stories and our cultural tradition. With them we have a chance to create and to express ourselves. They are one of the places we go to be ourselves and to become who we are going to be. There is no better place to smile, to sing, or to cry, than before our rug-hooking frame. It is the place to express yourself, and when you pour your emotions into your artwork, your emotions will appear upon the mat, and that, my friend, is Atlantic Canadian magic realism: it is the magic and the story in the mat.

Hook Yourself a Story

Our stories can be magical both as we tell them and as we hook them. Story has the power to transform an idea, to make people see things differently. Story has the power to change a life. I like to write, stringing words together like beads in pretty ways to get out a few ideas, but my real storytelling happens in my mats. It is a kind of interactive storytelling, and the magic happens both as I put my stories into my mats, and as others look at them and lend their own experience to them, creating their own stories. Sometimes I am very deliberate, but oftentimes I just make the mat and the story bursts out of me and onto the canvas.

When I wrote my first book about rug hooking, Dorothy Blythe at Nimbus Publishing suggested the title *Hook Me a Story*. When I heard it I wished I had thought of it myself. That is exactly what I was doing: hooking stories. She could see that the rugs I made had stories in them. The book focused on the history and method of mat-making, and storytelling was just something that she recognized in the mats. At times I had intentionally set out to tell a story with my mats, while other times the stories emerged as I made them. There have also been times when a visitor to the studio will tell me a story about one of my mats that is far more interesting than anything I had thought about that mat. I am open to the story in the mat, whether it is my own or someone else's. I find the perceptions and ideas of others as interesting as my own once the mat is completed.

The first step of storytelling is reflection and self-understanding. It is letting our memories come to the surface, and exploring those that do surface in a creative way so that we can make art with them. Storytelling in many ways is something that naturally arises in some rugs, while in others it is a deliberate choice and the rug-hooker puts a lot of effort into creating a storyboard. You can add elements that dictate the story in a clear, pictorial way. Stories come from both the maker and the person who views the rug. The experience that each person brings to the rug is what determines the story. So a rug-hooker might set out to tell one story, and when someone looks at the rug they see another. This is just part of making art; the maker loses control over what the world sees.

If you want to make story rugs, you must first know your own stories, the stories of your life. When I was in grade three or four, a teacher had us each create our autobiography with words and pictures in a Hilroy notebook. It was my first introduction to self-reflection, and the idea of getting to know myself. It was one of my favourite projects from all my school years. Today many people are writing their memoirs, not just the famous. It is a good exercise for any of us, to sit with ourselves and write our own story. The key I think is not to start out with the expected, just to be there with the pen, and see what happens. It is the only way the real stories will emerge. In our workshops at the studio we often have people get down on the floor and create a lifeline on a big sheet of newsprint. I ask them to write zero on one end of the line and their age on the other end of the line. I then suggest they draw symbols and make notations to mark the stories that have shaped their lives. I tell them to avoid the traditional rituals like graduations, marriage, births, and think more about smaller things. There are other ways of doing this, of course. You could journal or sketch them in a book, but whatever way you choose to approach it, the key to it is reflection. It may not be where you find your story mats. This initial reflection is an exercise in the importance and value of memory. It is a reminder to watch the memories, thoughts, and ideas about your past that emerge in your daily life. Take note of how handling a particular dish, or smelling lilac, triggers a story. You do

"Poppies on the Edge of Town." The poppies are a strong symbol of remembrance but they are also a rich and beautiful element in the landscape.

not need to engage in a search for an idea, rather you need to be open to the ideas that emerge naturally. Louise Bourgeois, the famous French sculptress, said that it is not the memory that we search for and mine that matters, it is what comes to the surface naturally that is important.

Symbols can be a huge part of storytelling in mats. I have so many symbols in my own life that mark the passage of a day. On my walks I count crows as my mother always did, superstitiously, seeking two as a symbol of joy. Big Cabbage roses are a symbol to me of the mat-makers that came before me, and the strong tradition in my family of making hooked rugs. Sunflowers are a symbol of my own seven acres, and they represent for me a sort of a tall, still guardian of joy, as joy I believe needs guarding. I plant a row each year, and again and again they keep emerging in my mats. I refuse to let them have been a trend, because they are too beautiful to dismiss. Big red poppies, like the ones in the rugs pictured in this chapter, remind me of my Uncle Donald, who as a young man in Newfoundland joined the British army during World War Two. He was on a ship off of Oran, in North Africa, that was torpedoed, and he was one of eighteen survivors on a boat of four hundred. He floated around in the water on a piece of wood, until he was picked up by a German ship and made a prisoner of war. He was shot in the elbow, and spent two years in hospital recovering. One day on a drive through New Brunswick, he wrote the story down for me in my sketchbook. I knew as he was writing it that it mattered. For forty years he lived as a bachelor in Brooklyn, New York, and worked on the high steel like so many Newfoundlanders. With their good sea legs they could navigate the narrow scaffolding high above that grand city. All my life, he came home in the summers and gave away money like he was rich when he wasn't. He was always a sharp dresser, with a nice suit and a fedora. He kept himself tickety boo. He was not sentimental about the war or Remembrance Day but nevertheless when I hook a poppy, it is so much more than a beautiful red flower. It is about generosity, and a showiness, and strength of spirit. Old-fashioned hand-carved net needles (page 130) are a symbol of my father, as are curls of smoke. These curls of smoke sometimes appear in my skies. The first time I saw this loose shape that gently shivered and shifted as it rolled up to the ceiling was in my father's curls of smoke. As a child I sat with him as he carved thin needles for knitting nets while smoke curled in thick white lines in his dark bedroom. He sold the needles, which once had been used for knitting nets and abundant in every fish store, in souvenir shops. Making souvenirs of what had previously been an essential tool foreshadowed the eventual collapse of this industry and way of life just a few decades later. These two simple shapes are a presence in many of my mats, symbols of my early life with Dad.

He was not sentimental about the war or Remembrance Day but nevertheless when I hook a poppy, it is so much more than a beautiful red flower.

Symbols are sometimes obvious, sometimes a foreshadowing, and sometimes rather obscure. In mat-making they can be as personal as you like. Some symbols are universal, but you can create your own personal and meaningful symbols. Most likely you already have them, they are just waiting to be acknowledged. Our lives are full of them, we meet them daily. Think a little about the symbols in your own life, and what they might represent. Keep your eyes wide open for new and old ones that begin to emerge. Can these be used in your mats? Sometimes symbols emerge naturally in our mats, and if we ask ourselves about them we will discover what they mean. They can also be added deliberately as part of our overall design, as part of the story we are creating. Oftentimes, symbols have to be adapted. You might have to find a simple way of drawing a more

"Poppies." I have a few big red poppies in my garden. Last year the first one bloomed on my birthday—a gift. The dark centres, purple and black, are so mysterious.

complex image so that it can be used as part of a design for a hooked mat. It will be important to find a way of drawing the idea simply with clear lines so that it is recognizable, beautiful, and easy to hook.

Sometimes when a story idea emerges, before you begin designing a rug, it is good to mull it over a little. You might want to write the story in your journal or sketchbook. You might try listing all the elements that you think are important. Writers often practice postcard stories, or stories that can fit on one typed sheet. Writing your story might lead to more ideas about the design you have begun. Of course once you have thought of everything, and explored the idea fully, the real challenge comes in paring it down, and finding the key and essential elements that are the most important and will best tell the story in your rug. Getting at the essence of an idea can be the most difficult thing to do. What is the central line of your story? Can you tell your story in one sentence? After playing with it, generating so much thought about it, it comes down to the notion of creating a single sentence to get at the essence of it. What idea do you want to

"Getting out of the Picture" is really a story about my son leaving childhood to become a man.

convey? Remember it is not what you want others to see that matters. What they see will be enhanced or restricted by their own minds. What matters is what you want to tell.

You might ask, why bother thinking about it so much if it is only a one-line story that matters? Sometimes that one line is already there for you, you know what to say, and the exploration is not necessary. But other times there is an underlying idea that only comes up when you fully explore the story. I find time thinking and pondering is time well spent. What is the sense of being human and coming to this huge gathering here on earth if you do not take the time to get to know yourself? We spend all kinds of energy getting to know others. If you want to make rugs as art, you need to put energy into getting to know yourself. It is your party and you are your own host, so be gracious.

Another ingredient in good storytelling is good listening. Often the stories of others are as interesting or more interesting than our own. But interesting is not enough; they need to inspire us. When you are listening to the stories of others you will sometimes find a story makes you feel something. This feeling is the key to inspiration.

Explore the stories of others, but remember that it is your reaction to them, the way they inspire you, that matters as you design the rug.

Story rugs do not have to be narrative. Often they are a chance to express a belief or an idea. To make them narrative you can make a rug a pictorial showing just what it is you want to convey, like the rug "Getting out of the Picture," (opposite) which reflects my son becoming a man and leaving his mother's hands. You can also use symbols or ideas to make the point, organizing them in a pleasing way, using all the elements of good design to create a pattern that is beautiful. I sometimes write a line of prose in rugs that relates to the story that is going on in my mind as I make the mat. I do not see the sense, really, in writing the obvious, as that should not be needed. For example, I would not write, "Uncle Jack in his boat" on my rug. I think it would be more meaningful to write a line from Uncle Jack's favourite song, or better still an eloquent sentence describing how I feel about Uncle Jack. The writing should not be an afterthought; it should be integrated into the overall design, and seen as part of the design that fits and belongs. Too often, words are thrown into rugs as a summation: in case you don't get the idea from the image, here it is in words. But if you use writing in rugs it should deepen the meaning of the rug for the maker, and awaken ideas in the viewer, rather than state the obvious. Once again, the words do not need to direct the viewer, or control their thinking about the rug, rather they should engage them and lead them to thoughts of their own. They should connect them to the mat as a whole, both visually and emotionally. There are also practical things to think of when writing in a rug. If you want to be able to read the words, then the hooking of the writing should be done tightly and neatly, in a colour that contrasts with the background so that it stands out (as shown in the rug "Thanks and Praise" on page 141). The colour of the writing should be part of the colour planning for the whole rug. You may need to hook the writing in two rows, or more if the mat is large, so that it stands out well. The curves in the writing might need to be accentuated by hooking them a little more solidly.

I almost always need at least two rows of hooking to make the writing readable. Otherwise, the script is thin and gets lost in the background of the mat. Writing in rugs can be beautiful, and will enhance the story as long as it adds to the overall design and deepens the meaning of the piece.

The story in your mat could happen in the border or the main part of the rug. Borders are a strong tradition in mat-making and a lot can be shown in them. I enjoy creating them because they act as another layer of meaning in the mat. They do not have to be purely decorative. You can choose an idea to express in the border, and use symbols to get your point across. Borders are also an excellent way to integrate writing into the mat. I will often use them to write a few lines of prose, but when I do this I still try to add some decorative elements, such as leaves, scrolls, or flowers, so that the border has something to rely upon for beauty. I have an old daybook that lists flowers and plants and their symbolic meaning, and I often refer to that to find a plant leaf or flower to include in the border that will act as a symbol for the story in the rest of the rug. The border of the rug "Getting out of the Picture" (page 82) enhances an already complete scene without interfering with it.

Beauty intrigues, and intrigue is one of the first levels of storytelling. I remember years ago I made a rug of a woman holding a fish, and in the background was a wood stove, and a portion of a male figure sitting on a chair. As I was making the rug it was just an image, but as I hooked, the story came about of how she worked in the fish plant and had brought this fish home to fry. Her husband had moved with resettlement and there was no work. As I told it to a visitor in the studio, she said, "Ah, that's why he's half a man." It wasn't consciously why I made him half a man, but it made a better story. I made him half a man because it fit with the composition. It was a decision about beauty. If you let it, the story just comes. You don't have to create all the narrative; you just have to show it as you imagine it to be, as beautifully as you can, and the story will follow.

When I am telling stories in mats I always choose beauty over truth. First and foremost, what I am doing is making a mat, and beauty is my main concern, so if in the story the boat is red, in mine it might be red, or it might be brown. I have no guilt about this, because I want my rug to be as beautiful as I can make it. The real nature of story for me is fiction anyway. I value the truth, but I know it is not always necessary

"Under a Paisley Sky." There she is, so happy and thankful, in praise of the day.

or relevant. As in life, in my mats the truth is sometimes no help, so I let it go. Remember that the word *story* does not mean that what is being said is true. Sometimes when I am making a mat I do not even start with a story, but in hooking it a story emerges. This is really obvious when I hook my big-boned girls. As I make each of these tiny portraits of women, I imagine who they are, what they might do. They each emerge with their own story.

In making a rug beautiful, I want to draw in the viewer. You do not have to put a ton of things into the mat to get your point across. The old adage "a picture paints a thousand words" remains relevant. It is even better if those thousand words are different for every person who sees the picture. They might find it beautiful or haunting; it does not matter. It only matters that they are moved by it and find some story inside themselves that ties them to the piece. I love watching people react to my mats and listening to what they have to say about them. Each person has a tale to tell me, and from that tale I learn about them as well as about the mat they are looking at. Our stories are our own, but we all know that once they are told and retold, they become transformed into something bigger than us. Whatever was in our hearts and minds transforms itself into a piece of art.

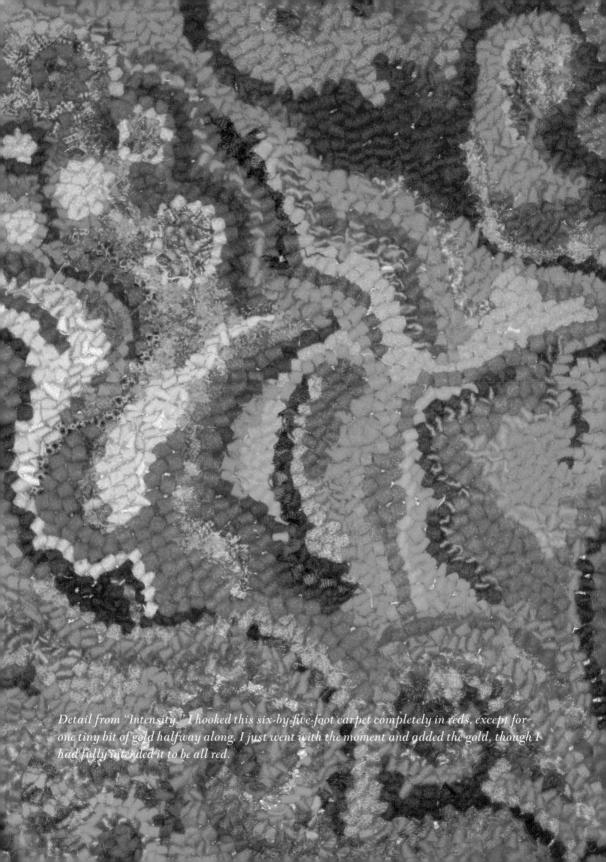

Detail from "Intensity." I hooked this six-by-five-foot carpet completely in reds, except for one tiny bit of gold halfway along. I just went with the moment and added the gold, though I had fully intended it to be all red.

CHAPTER 5
Creativity and Spirit

Small Matters

A rt is nothing without creativity and spirit. It is these things that bring art to life, and it is in tapping these things that we are able to transform our own lives. We learn to live more generously through them and to be kinder to ourselves, enabling us to be kinder to the world around us. You can use your mats to tell stories, to say a few prayers, to meditate, and to contemplate.

You can also use your mats to soothe yourself in hundreds of different ways. Handwork inevitably becomes mind work. In creating, we believe that beauty matters, and so we bring it forth. We also know that small matters, and we use our rug-hooking to change our own little worlds, one loop at a time.

To be creative, you need to let your spirit speak, and you need to let go of yourself. You need to loosen your mind, your conscious and critical thought, and you need to let your hands move freely. I understand when people tell me that they can't let go, get lost in the rhythm of the mat. I too struggle with the same things in different ways. Getting lost in something, finding that place where the hand and mind are working together through you, rather than through your labour, is a place of prayer. Inspiration turns our conscious thought into little more than the rhythm of what we are doing, the whoosh of the hand meeting the mat. It is the words spilling forward when you've no idea where they came from. It is the image appearing before you. Inspiration is a kind of a blessing, and a kind of a meditation. It is the meeting of the hand and the art coming through the spirit. Inspiration is ethereal, the stuff of the spirit. It is like sitting and waiting for the muse to visit. The key, of course, is you need to be committed, there with hook in hand, on a steady basis, because the muse might visit anytime, and the more often you are ready for her, the more often she might come.

I once visited an art gallery and the owner spoke about one of her painters. She said, "He gets up and he paints every day. None of this waiting to be inspired...He works and the paintings happen." When she was interviewed in the *Halifax Herald* after winning the CBC poetry prize, Sue Goyette, a Nova Scotia writer, said she shows up to write every day, and sometimes the muse doesn't show, but she feels good that at least she always shows up. I loved that little comment. It reflects her commitment to the process. She is there. She works hard. Even if the spirit in her is not willing to release that much, she is there, at the desk. As rug-hookers, not everything we make will be a work of art. Some of our work should be tea cozies, some should have the life beaten out of them by the front door. What is the harm in wearing something out? Only some things should outlast us. But we should make things every day. We should sit with ourselves, walk with ourselves, and use our hands in the studio every day, every chance we get.

Twyla Tharp, the American modern dancer, wrote a book on creativity called *The Creative Habit*, and in that book there is one real premise, that creativity is a habit. You form that habit, carry out the work, and you will be creative. Create a ritual for yourself that allows you to get to a place where you can make the rug, write the words, dance the dance. Engage yourself in making things and you will learn something new from each thing you make. I believe that the more you make, the more you will learn. Others feel that being prolific is not important. It can be true, no doubt. Look at Alistair MacLeod: one book of short stories and one novel. Neither would I want to have missed. Both were exquisite. My guess, though, is he was always writing, always reading, always at his craft, always learning.

When I first started seeking out other artists to visit in their studios I was amazed to find that so many good artists are not into being artists as we imagine them, or as books and the media portray them. Most of the good artists I have met over the years are practical, hardworking people. They dress plainly. They eat healthily. They don't drink too much. They make a lot of art, and they support themselves doing it. I have little time for pretense, so this discovery pleased me. I found they were inspired by their surroundings, whatever they were. They make compromises of all kinds. They have open minds. They look for ideas because they know that nothing is more beautiful than an idea. They know that once they have an idea they can take it and form it and chip away at it and add to it, and they can make something with it. A good artist wants to transform ideas into something of their own. They have come up with a practical response to their search for meaning, and have chosen to make stuff. When I start a mat, I just let it flow, and I tell the truth as I see it, knowing you might see

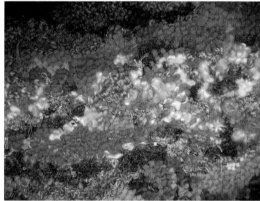

Details from field rugs. These are the kind of rugs where you have to be open to the moment, letting one wool come freely after another.

it differently and that's okay. I don't know how to get you to put your spirit into your work. I can only speak for myself, and how I do it. I hope that you can get some glimmer of sense from what I have to say.

I know that if you allow yourself to get lost in something, if you are able to get lost in your mat-making, if you stop the constant evaluation of your work, then there is a better possibility that exciting things will happen with it. Whenever I start thinking that I must live up to something, that this rug I am working on must be better than the last, I hinder myself. I need to forget about what I am doing to do it well. That is what allows me the freedom to express myself fully. If my ego gets in the way, and it sometimes does, like when I start thinking "I must make art," both me and my work, and everyone who knows me, suffer. Stuffiness is a problem and a barrier. Simply put, I must keep saying and feeling, "I must make rugs." The idea of art in hooked mats should not be a barrier to us. It should just be a side effect of us doing something as well and as beautifully as we can. We need to make rugs. We need to not have to say we're making art. If it is art it will be art.

Whenever I start thinking that I must live up to something, that this rug I am working on must be better than the last, I hinder myself.

I think the real goal in every part of life for me is to do what I do, and do it as well as I can. I have said that from the beginning of my career in rug-hooking. Every time I say "career in rug-hooking," I think it is an oxymoron. I am still excited about what I do. I learned that I have to focus on doing what I do and cut out all the distractions that I can. Over the years I have had many calls from people in rug-hooking worried about the way others are doing things and how it reflects on them. All I ever say is "Do what you know, what you do, and do it as well as you can. Don't worry about what someone else is doing." I do try to watch what everyone else is doing. I do that because I am interested in people, but I try not to care too much, and I try not to get involved because I know that my family, my work, and my community take all the energy I have.

To create you have to believe in yourself and in your own life. Last year a woman called me and said, "My sister said to tell you that when she wakes up in the middle of the night and can't get back to sleep she goes down and reads your website." I said, "Tell your sister I said that when she wakes up in the middle of the night she should wake up her husband, never mind reading my website." We both had a great laugh, but my message was that her sister

Anne Hallet, a rug-hooking artist from Ontario, inspired me with this gift of her hand-dyed skeins. Her artful approach to rug-hooking has also inspired me.

should nurture her own life, what was right in front of her, or beside her, whatever the case may be. We need to believe in the value and importance of our own lives, and the way we do things, and what we have around us. We need to sit on our own front stoops to find ourselves first before we set off on some transcontinental journey. The way home is in your own breath and your own stillness.

I spend a lot of time on mundane things. I like to cut wool some days in the studio. I like to tear up wool shirts for the bins. I like to hook traditional hit-and-miss mats. I like the practical aspects of keeping a studio running, of gathering stuff up for orders, making sure there are extra paper towels. I like to pick up the printing. If I hired some fancy consultant, she would say, "Those things should be hired out at such and such an hour, and you should be making art, writing, or something that only you can do." But for me, it is in the mundane that I can find myself, as long as I do not allow it to bury me. It is in doing the mundane, the necessary chores of a life in fibre, that ideas spring forth like a snowdrop in the spring. Sometimes the dull stuff is a rest for the brain, a siesta. The other day I cleaned my studio from top to bottom. I sorted through the wool. I handled every piece I had there. I took all the scraps and sorted them by colour, and

"In the Flock." This woman is enjoying the moment. She is not afraid to feel the wind.

cut them and bagged them. Nothing happened, but I felt good, and it enabled me to step away for a time. So what I know is that in order to stay creative it is important not to pressure myself to be creative all the time. Be creative when you feel creative. When you don't, clean the oven.

I keep my focus and I believe in the way I do things. It is not always easy but it is always easier than doing things you do not want to be doing. I say no to all kinds of beautiful opportunities. I miss out sometimes on experiences and meeting new, wonderful people. It means I shut out some things that would benefit me. It means I don't always give others what they want or make them happy. It means I am sometimes selfish. That's what focused people are like. On the one hand their focus delights you; on the other it might disappoint you. I grew up with a father who taught me this. A good lesson, it was hard learned, and more valuable to me than I might have ever imagined. My father did what he wanted, sometimes at the expense of my mother and I. As a child I found this very difficult, but experiencing it has made me a stronger person and a better artist.

To be an artist, I need to have faith in myself. In the beginning the faith was built upon a wing and a prayer, and a bit of bravado. Now I sometimes build it on the fact that I have had success in the past. That is encouraging. Though when it comes right down to the nitty-gritty and I'm feeling kind of shaky about a new idea, or a complex rug, I just sit down wherever I am, hold my chin in my hands, look down at my sneakers, and think, "You know, I like my mats. They're kind of pretty." That is what gives me the real strength to go on and create new things. I love what I do and I believe in what I do. I think hooked rugs are beautiful. I love the feeling of making them. I believe that making them is good for my spirit, as it is good for the spirit of anyone who likes to make them. I don't take it too seriously. When I question myself I know that I just need to make the mat, get back at it, and forget the foolishness. I always think that you know you've made a really great mat when you can give yourself a shiver with your own work.

That shiver only happens every once in a while. Right rare it is, let me tell you. I remember the first time it happened. It was the rug that I eventually sold to the Art Gallery of Nova Scotia for their permanent collection. I looked at it and I thought, "I don't think I really made that." It was the first time I understood that art is made by your spirit as much as it is made by your hands. It was a revelation for me. Now every once in a while I get that feeling, and I want to do a little dance because of the way the wools are working together, or the way the thing looks all together. "The shiver" is a wonderful motivation. It is one of the most pleasant feelings I have ever experienced. It is also the foundation of my confidence. I know I can get it again because I got it before. I am me, and that is all I am, and it is all I have to give the mats. No big fancy stuff, just make the mat.

Focus on your work, and mine yourself and your environment for ideas. Remember that small things matter, that small things are beautiful. Annie Dillard knew this when she wrote *Pilgrim at Tinker Creek* when she was in her twenties. She wrote a book about her own relationship with a little creek near her house, and she examined every tiny aspect of the creek as she observed it. She won the Pulitzer Prize. What good is it to diminish the small, to

Detail from "Intensity." Sometimes one little area of a rug is enough to say, "That was worth making."

disregard the simple? All things are built upon one another.

Little children know the importance of small, and we know the importance of small when we observe them. Small things can make huge differences. I think of my own life as small, really. I live in a plain house, on the edge of a small town, and I make mats, but I believe that small things matter, and so I matter, and my stories matter, and my mats matter. I often hear people minimize their own experiences as uninteresting. I think they are uninteresting because they are unexplored. None of our stories are that unique and interesting. Most story lines have been told and retold. It is your spirit that you add to it that makes it unique. It is the only unique part in any story. It is what makes your story your own. Your spirit, your individuality, is the gift that you bring to the world when you are born, it is the gift you offer your friends and family every day, the gift you offer to your rugs, and finally it is the gift that lingers after you have gone from the world, and remains in the hearts of those whose lives you have influenced. Believe that you are small, but that small matters. Someone once said to me that your spirit is what remains in the room after you have walked out of it. Our spirit is bigger than us, and if we stop trying to direct and control it, and let it lead us as it has the power to do, our stories will be bigger than we can know.

I often hear people minimize their own experiences as uninteresting. I think they are uninteresting because they are unexplored.

I always think of the time I asked Ghita Levin about her childhood. Ghita is a renowned potter in Atlantic Canada. I had imagined with a name like Ghita, and a long-time career as such a fantastic potter who now lives on a homestead outside Port Elgin, she would tell me that she grew up as a wandering waif whose parents carried her aboard small sailing vessels on fantastic voyages. I expected a story. What she said was, "I grew up in Ottawa and mostly hung out at the mall." I laughed. What that told me was that Ghita created her own life, her own story, in her work, and that her beautiful work is her real story. Ghita let her spirit speak. Her hands told her story with clay and form. She has mined both herself and the natural world for understanding. What she told me was that her real story was within her. It was not about experiences, or travels, but was about her relationship with the natural world. Her story was in her spirit.

I have since found that when people talk at dinner parties about great travels and places they have been, I am not always all that interested. It depends on the real story. I don't want to know about luggage, tourist destinations, or restaurants. What I am interested in is journeys. I want to know what happened to these people, inside themselves, what was revealed to them as they travelled. I have found that some people can drive to Springhill and come back profoundly altered, while others can go to the Himalayas and come back with little more than a list of place names, and the address of a good guide. Sometimes journeys are small but fascinating. Others are long, maybe even arduous, but not very compelling.

Hooking alone, letting your thoughts flow freely, is a gift to yourself. It will uncover the richness of your interior self if you want it to. Some people don't want to explore themselves. They have no need, and that is fine also. One of the most wonderful stories I have heard over the years is about Brenda Head's mother. Brenda was visiting the studio, and I was telling her what I just told you, that rug-hooking gives me time to think. She told me that her mother once told her that she likes really complicated knitting patterns because she has to focus so much on the pattern that her mind does not wander to all kinds of old worries. I like this idea as much as I like my own idea about why I hook. Rug-hooking can be used to get to know yourself, but it can also be used to save you from yourself. As much as it is a chance to get to know who you are, it is also a chance to lose yourself in colour, pattern, texture, and design.

Once years ago, my friend Lynda Burke gave me a little life lesson. She dropped into the house as I was about to go on a trip. I said to her, "You know, since I had kids, I think I have become afraid of flying." She said, "You're not afraid of flying, you're afraid of dying. That's what we're all afraid of. No one is really afraid of flying, but we are all afraid of dying." I have thought about what she said to me for years, and I think that I have discovered that the real wisdom in her words is not the flying and dying wisdom, which is pretty good in itself, but it is the fact that we all have fears, and sometimes we use one fear to cover up another. Sometimes the idea of really putting your spirit into your mat, and laying it bare, is scary. What if it does not work out? What if it is not good? What if no one likes it? Worse again, what if you don't like it yourself? You cannot always be the best judge of your own work. I have made mats I do not like, but they tell the truth. They tell the story without my approval. You can let it be, but you can always start over. You can always make another mat, better than the last one. You know on one level you have to

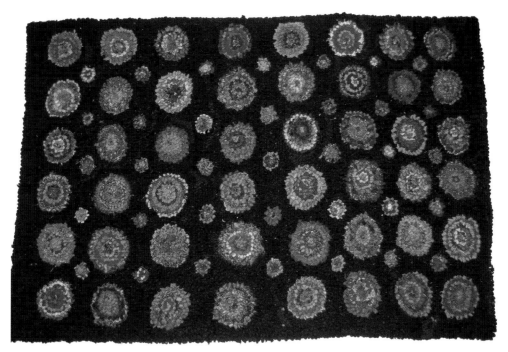

"Blue around Midnight" is a play on the idea of blues music and late nights at a roadhouse.

think you are really important, important enough to bother putting your whole self into something. On the other hand you have to think that you are not all that important, and that if you waste time, or mess up, it really is not going to matter all that much.

I know that the more time you spend with the hook in your hand the more you will learn. I know that many people get great joy out of hooking with groups but I also know that you need to hook alone sometimes in order to become passionate about it, in order for the art of rug-hooking to emerge. It is a meditative and creative activity. It will give you one thing if you give it your full attention, and another if you just play around with it. Both are rewarding. I have sat down at the frame angry and gotten up forgiving. I have learned the truth about myself, both good and bad. I have learned that in a kind of way, my hook and frame are my home. I belong with them, and they belong with me.

Creative Rug-hooking

For many people rug-hooking is a bit more than a hobby; they see it as a part of who they are. They have chosen to hook rugs because it suits them. Women like the social camaraderie around getting together to hook in groups. They like the tradition surrounding it, and the fact that you can recycle old clothes into an expressive art form. Often people hook for years, and once again it is being passed on from generation to generation. Over a lifetime people create a huge collection of rugs that they have made themselves. Some of these are hooked from patterns bought at supply shops, but in most collections you will also find a few that were created from scratch, and designed by the rug-hooker. More and more people are approaching rug-hooking with a freedom of expression and a genuine desire to use their hook to show the world who they are.

Once we settle into rug-hooking, the desire to be creative about it follows closely behind. We feel the need to play with it, be adventuresome, and see how far we can take it. Just how beautiful or how exciting can a mat be? That is a question that has yet to be answered because the resurgence in rug-hooking is relatively new. There has been an art quilting movement for many, many years. People have explored quilting the way painters have explored paint. The contemporary movement towards art rugs is just a baby in comparison. This is a nice place to be, really, because as children we look upon everything with fresh eyes. With the exception of a strong tradition of the craft of rug-hooking in our culture we don't have a lot of guidelines. We are free to explore this craft, be creative with it, and bring it to the level of art.

I know that when I am really creative I am not planning so much as responding, so I don't plan out my whole mat with a colour scheme. Instead I create a basis of two or three colours that I want to work from. I try to close my eyes and imagine what the mat might look like

"Black Birds." My relationship with crows continues in my work, but it changes and evolves as I change.

when done. In that visualization I try to recreate the colour theme. I don't jot down the colour of every item in the mat. Instead I pull the few colours from my wool stash that convey that feeling I am after, the two or three colours that were most prominent in the visualization. All creative work takes a little planning, but you have to be willing to change plans midstream, and be open to the fact that each step in the creative process alters the possibilities for the next step. If you over-plan, it is hard to let go and be responsive. Responsiveness is the heart of playfulness, and playfulness is at the heart of creativity.

Being playful is also a necessary part of nurturing your creativity. Being playful does not mean you have to wear toe socks with multicoloured stripes or put pigtails in your hair. That I think of more as playacting. Playfulness is a way of being that comes with a softness of heart and, some might say, of mind. This winter I lay around and read for hours at a time, and pretended that I was semi retired. I just let myself be and tempered my expectations for productivity and usefulness. I did not think of time as something that had to be managed, and I never let myself think that time reading, walking, or doing yoga was time away from something else. It was just time to play, and play is as good for the mind as work. When you hook a rug, the playful mind really comes alive as you look at all the different wools and other fabrics that are available to you. There are endless colours and textures that can make our hands dance with glee as we thread them through our fingers. I don't see any room to limit ourselves to any one type of fabric, or any one set of colour tones. Why would we? We are only closing off possibilities when we do this. Feel free to use any fabric or texture you like in your mats. Play with fabric and see what it does when you hook it. Learn what you can do with it. You own your mat, you own your hands. Don't let anyone tell you how to use them. Explore the world of colour and texture as if you were a child. Who knows what you can do with what is available to you.

Discovering what's available to you means that you start becoming very observant of the materials around you. Is there a knitter in your area who has tons of tiny bits of wool that are of no use to her? Is there anyone making any kind of textile that would have scraps they no longer need, and are of little value to them? Where are the secondhand stores in your neighbourhood? See what they have an abundance of that might work for you. I don't just go to the skirt bin looking for wool anymore. I have discovered that silk shirts, sweaters, and scarves can be used well in my work. I like soft angora sweaters, and have sometimes come home with armloads of velour. The secondhand store is a big box of sixty-four crayons, and if you are playful enough you'll try every colour in the box.

Try hooking a small rug without any pattern drawn on it. Take a selection of beautiful wools, and hook them freeform onto a backing, not following any design. This will give you a chance to loosen up and get used to the idea that sometimes there are no mistakes.

A few years ago I took a month off hooking and when I went back to it I created a hooked rug of squares called "Gone Mod." I thought I was just using up bits but it turned out to be one of my favourite mats, and what I thought would be very traditional turned out to be very contemporary. It was the letting go, the playfulness, that allowed that rug to happen.

"Gone Mod." In this playful mat I was exploring an old tradition but it ended up looking thoroughly modern.

"Don't turn your back on me" is a rug about friendship and relationships, the way we count on each other but drive each other crazy.

CHAPTER 6

People and Community

Darkening the Door: The Art of Visiting

In our own houses we get to be truly ourselves. This is the place where people can see us as we truly are. It should be the place we are safe and comfortable, a place where we can tell the truth about ourselves without having to say a word. There was a time when we met each other in our kitchens instead of in coffee shops. We still do, of course, but in some ways visiting has become a bit of a lost art. People find it harder and harder to drop in on each other, especially unannounced. We have gotten into the habit of retreating in front of our big TVs and shutting out the rest of the world. Some of us are starting to believe that an evening spent on Facebook is an evening spent with friends. Real visiting, sitting in each other's company in our own homes, is how we can come to know each other more fully. Seeing someone in their own place, with the life they have built around them, is a comfort as you come to know them. It is a way of really knowing them. It offers us a chance to reach new depths of understanding about each other, and about ourselves. Sometimes it just offers us a chance to laugh and be foolish.

It takes some courage in a society that is ruled by daytimers to drop in on someone. Sometimes I like to work on themes in my rugs, and the art of visiting is an idea I explored, creating a series of rugs for a show. As I made the mats, I thought a great deal about the nature of visiting, and through it I learned some things about myself. I discovered that sometimes in having a visit with someone else I leave with a new understanding of myself. Often we set out

"Feeding Men." Food is an important part of visiting—sharing what you have, feeding guests.

to visit someone, thinking of it as something we do for that person. I know now that it is something that I do for myself. I learned that visiting is about more than a cup of tea and a biscuit. It is about deepening respect and understanding for each other. By constantly babysitting ourselves with electronic toys, we sacrifice our soulfulness. We learn very little about ourselves from them, and even less about others. Real relationships happen when we meet each other across the table and tell the truth about ourselves, when together we mull over our circumstances and ideas. Visits are about conversations, both the ones you have with the company you visit, and the ones you have with yourself long after the visit has ended.

When I visited the Placentia area of Newfoundland several years ago, I went to see Winnie Leonard, my childhood neighbour. By her door was the same press-back chair I had sat in thirty-five years before as a girl, waiting for her daughter Mary to come play. It was once painted with dark red oil paint, the colour of a brick, but with a shine. That day Winnie reminded me of how my father used to stand with his foot propped up on our white rail fence, cigarette in one hand, cup of coffee in the other, and look out at the bay before he went to work in the morning. She said, "I look out that front window and I still see him dere sure. It was like yesterday. Where does time go?" Winnie was not making simple conversation.

She was truthfully wondering and marvelling at the idea of time disappearing. She was asking the deep philosophical question of where time goes. What had happened to my father, the fence, the moment of looking out to sea? What had happened to the time that had passed, slipped through our experience, and settled only in our minds? I knew she wondered these things like I did. Winnie and I only see each other once in a long while, but I feel a kinship with her. It is a beautiful visit when you leave with a deeper understanding of your neighbour, having shared an unanswered question that lingers in your mind, knowing neither you nor she could answer it but that it torments the both of you. It is enough to share the question.

Visits also trigger memory. What one person remembers triggers your own unconscious memories. I had not remembered my father standing the way she described. Yet, later that week I caught myself lifting my leg to settle my foot upon a stone wall and look out at the water. I leaned my elbow over my knee. It was a completely unconscious act, but as I did it I felt a physical memory of my father. I was standing exactly the way he did and suddenly I remembered looking out my own window and seeing him thirty-five years before. The memory did not come back to me through my mind but through blood, and bone, and physical movement, and it was all triggered by my visit with Winnie. Our memory and consciousness is bigger when we are part of a community that remembers things with us. I knew more about myself, my father, and Winnie because I bothered to drop in on her. It brought me to another place in myself.

I enjoy reading fiction, nature writing, non-fiction, and philosophy. I have learned a great deal from reading but I only ever remember a few elements from each book. It seems I read a book full of amazing ideas and I can completely forget most of them, and reread it again as if it were new a year later. Yet when I learn a little bit of philosophy from another person as I visit them in the comfort of their own home it seems to stay with me. One night I was having a beer with a friend, Phillip Burke. We were in his living room, and he was watching golf on television. I was curled up on the end of the couch and he was sitting in an old beat-up recliner. Phillip is an electrician who wears a baseball cap, golfs, hunts, and drinks beer. Unlike the stereotype, Phillip is also a smart and sensitive person. We were talking about life. He had recently lost his wife, Lynda, who had died suddenly. Our families were good friends. Phillip had been the best man at our wedding. Lynda was there when I had my babies. That night I was just checking in and we were chatting as the golf flashed on TV. Somehow through the course of the conversation, in reference to both his wife and daughter, he said, "You know, it is one thing to love someone, but it is another thing altogether to be loved." He knew there was a jarring difference between the two, and that loving someone made you feel one thing, but being loved by someone made you more than you thought you could be. They were clearly different experiences. I agreed, naturally, and we continued to talk, but that little statement has resonated with me now for three years. That simple conversation over a beer resounds in my mind as I walk, as I write, and often even as I talk. The power of darkening a door, of meeting someone on their own ground, in their own place, can be profound. I remember that conversation in all kinds of contexts, and it is one of the tenets I try to abide by in my relationships, as very rarely are we able to offer perfect and equal amounts of love to each other. I remember that even if I love and am not loved back equally, it is worth a lot. Sometimes being loved myself more than I have loved back has made me better. These unequal doses of love, that we give and receive, make us what we are. Philip's few words, said as he sat in his beat-up recliner, reminded me of the power of visiting someone on their own piece of ground. Quiet conversations can lead you to understanding. You'll say things in your own chair that you would not say in a coffee shop downtown.

Of course, good visits like this can happen wherever you are comfortable. As a child I often went up on the north side of Argentia American Naval base, passing the artillery bunkers to fish trout in the ponds there with my father. It was a regular Saturday trip. On my last visit back I went on a hike there with my friend Tish and

Argentia, Newfoundland: A scene I had not seen for years.

another artist, Christopher Newhook from Placentia. Christopher, Tish, and I went down in the early evening to hike on a trail that the development association had cut out on the bog that overlooked the bay. I had been there before as a child but had only vague memories. The most interesting thing that I discovered that night was that my understanding of the landscape, my feeling for it, did not have to be in my conscious memory. When I came over a little hill and looked out towards Fox Harbour, I saw a scene that I had not seen for years, and that I had forgotten. Immediately I thought of a rug I had made that winter prior to coming. It was inspired by the scene that was in front of me, but I had not until that moment consciously recognized that. I thought that I had made the rug from

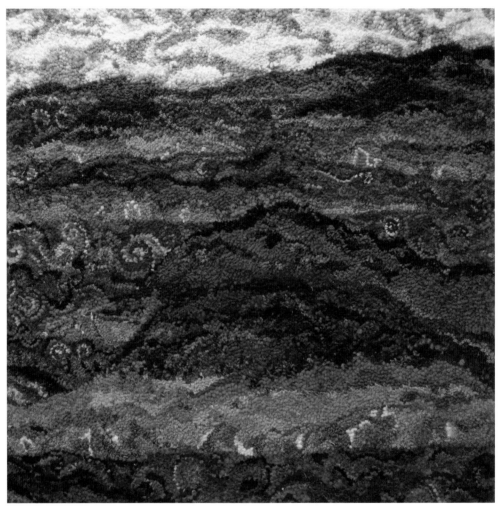

"All Around the Islands." I thought I made this rug as an imaginary place, only to find out it was very much like the view from Argentia that I was so familiar with as a child.

imagination, when in fact I had made it from memory, from those Saturday trouting expeditions with my father. That evening sewed up a lifetime of experiences for me. I had memories in my unconscious that had already been knit into my mats. It confirmed for me that the landscape of my childhood, the fishing trips across the bog, the hills that I lay upon and looked up at the sky from were more deeply woven into me than I ever knew. I was bound to it whether I was treading upon it or not. So visiting for me is also about visiting place, and cultivating a relationship with the landscape.

I grew up in a house where you were encouraged to ponder and think. Not in a formal way, but there were books around, my father told me to question things, and I was left on my own a lot. My parents were plain people; both had very little education. My mother finished grade seven, and my father grade ten, but they could speak truths in a single sentence that I have read as chapters in books. I used to sit with my mother, visiting her as she tried to steal a nap. I once asked her about love, and if she loved my father. She said to me, "Deanne, what is love?" A very short sentence, but it is one that relates to every complex relationship that ever existed. I still remember the day she said it, the look on her face, the way she tilted her head back, and the fact that she was wearing a neatly pressed pale green shirt of my father's. She was not quite sure what love was and she could not fill my head with fluff. She was not able to because her experience would not let her. Plain and simple, she gave me just the facts, as she saw them, in the form of a question. This happened just because I was there, because we made a habit of being present with each other.

My parents and I left Newfoundland when I was sixteen and going into grade eleven. For me it felt as if I was being torn away from everything I felt comfortable with and it led me to have the strong attachment that many artists have with their home place, their formative landscape. I have lived in Nova Scotia since I was sixteen, not very far away but an absolutely different place. I did go back to Newfoundland for a couple of years to attend university but I never settled there again. For years I visited once or twice a year, but after my second child was born it was eight years before I went back. It was on this visit and subsequent others that I really got to thinking about my relationship with Newfoundland and the landscape. Newfoundland has influenced my work so much, and leaving it may have had a hand in developing my passion for mat-making. It may have given me something to say, and perhaps a way to say it. Yet, as much as I feel that the landscape belongs to me, it is only in a visual kind of way. It is only in memory. I have created a life somewhere else. That life has strengthened me and nurtured me, also making me whatever it is that I am. I have not committed myself to the place I grew up, the place that formed the essence of who I am, yet that landscape and my love for the way of life I remember there haunts me and infiltrates my art. It is at the very core of a great deal of my work. There are times, from afar, when I have sudden, passing pangs of guilt about no longer being a part of the landscape I long for. Yet when I go back to visit I realize that I no longer belong in the same way. I know now that when I go back to Newfoundland, I am visiting place, and I am visiting myself. Most of the people I know I have to visit in the graveyard. I walk down the road I grew up on, and people search my face for recognition. Once in a while someone remembers and I am comforted. I know I no longer matter to the place because I am not there. It is only the place that matters to me. Newfoundlanders have always left. I remind myself that even my great-great-grandfather left Ireland. The leaving did not begin with me.

Visiting is more than dropping in on a neighbour. It is also about visiting place. There are times when I need to go back to Newfoundland just to see the barrens, and there are times I need to go to the marsh to once again meet the Bay of Fundy. Place shapes us and sinks into our being, making us who we are. I belong to those landscapes that I have lived on for years at a time, even when they no longer belong to me. They become part of my spirit and my art is just my spirit made real in the form of hooked rugs.

In using my rugs to explore the idea of visiting and what it means, I came up with a lot of ideas and triggered memories I did not even know I had. Looking at something in depth, and exploring it in every way possible creates a new relationship with that idea. The idea itself changes and morphs, and you begin to understand it in new ways. I like to use my rug-hooking to explore ideas fully,

"Visiting on the way from Church" reflects women's conversations about what is happening around them, the stories they share in their community.

making mats about different aspects of an idea. I enjoy creating a show that allows the mats to be strengthened by each other, as an idea is played with. I can say that my values about the importance of visiting have been stated clearly because I spent a year creating images around the same idea. I have said it in pictures, and as people have looked at the mats I hope they have been reminded of who or what they themselves needed to go and see.

Hooking People

I f I could hook a face, exactly as it is, there would be no need for me to photograph it. If I could take the memory that lies behind my eyelids when I close them and think of all my beloveds, and stamp it exactly onto burlap, I would not be an artist but a magician. I would be a genius, perhaps, but the little soul that lives in me, and only wishes to show how I feel about the people around me, the people I grew up loving, would be lost. I would be lost. As it is, when I hook people I can only hook my idea of them, the idea of them that lives in me.

Recently, I called an old friend who lives in Labrador City to see if he could round me up a pair of snowshoes. I told him that in my show "The Art of Visiting" I had made a rug, of him wearing his black coat, called "The Boy from Point Verde." He said, "My mountie coat," and I said, "Yeah, that's the one." I sent him a picture of the rug and told him, "It doesn't look like ya, but it feels like ya." It is the best way that I can explain hooking a portrait. To me it is more important that the rug feel like someone than look like them. I work in a primitive style, but like my old anthropology professor once said about what were then called primitive societies: "Even the most primitive are very complex." I feel that way about primitive rug-hooking: if you want to do it creatively, there is a lot to learn.

Hooking people is one kind of impressionistic hooking. We are using wide cuts of cloth and hooking them onto burlap, so it is very difficult, if not impossible, to capture exact likenesses. I have always striven to capture the essence of the person I want to create a portrait of. To do this I need to get across an idea in the simplest way possible. For me it is often the tilt of someone's head, the style of clothing, hair colour and texture, height, and body shape that will help me capture them. I think of them not so much as portraits, though they are in a way, but more as memory rugs. I use this medium to capture what I remember about a person, so in that way they are sometimes more about me than about the person being hooked. It is my expression of how I see them.

The biggest mistake I have made over the years is creating people that have a stiffness about them that seems unnatural. I have learned that this happens in the outlining of the person. I would hook the outline very tight and close together, and as a result the person would look rigid, like a standing corpse, and would have to be pulled out and reworked after I finished the mat. When you

"The Boy from Point Verde" captures the essence of my old friend Earl McGrath and the way he looked as a teenager. I did not worry about being exact; I wanted to convey a feeling.

hook people, your outlining should be loose and in a narrow width. I usually use number 6 strips for this, and prefer a lightweight skirt wool. The outline defines the shape of the person, so it is very important. I often choose black, navy, dark grey, or any other dark colour that approximates black. I like to use solids for this. When I outline I skip extra holes so that the outline does not become a solid heavy black line that overtakes the image. Your outline should be the bones of your person, a structure, there but unseen. I do not often outline faces or hair. If the people are very small in the context of a larger mat they might not be outlined at all. You can create the impression of people by hooking them without outlines, and then hooking the background around them quite tightly, to give them extra shape.

When you decide to create a portrait of someone, start thinking about their physical attributes, habits, or mannerisms. Ask yourself, what are a few qualities that sum them up? Take these few qualities and try to capture them. If you are using a picture, put it away for a few days and think about what you remember of the picture. Use

"Bathing Beauties." I have hooked women in flamboyant suits many times over the years. I think the bandanas and purse reflect how so many of us are slightly uncomfortable coming out in our bathing suits.

what you remember to begin your design.

Pictures are both an excellent tool and a great encumbrance when it comes to designing rugs. If you cannot draw, you can put an overhead projector sheet over the picture and trace the image. You can then use a projector to project the image onto a piece of backing pinned on the wall, and trace the pattern onto your backing this way. Another option is to have the picture enlarged at a printer. You can then use wedding tulle, available at fabric stores, to trace the image. Put the tulle over your backing and trace the image again, and the ink will seep onto your backing to create a pattern. These methods are both reliable, but often they will result in stiff-looking people, and it will be evident that they have been traced. They lack feeling. If you create a pattern this way, be sure to go over the lines before you hook them, softening them a bit. People do not have many straight lines. We are mostly lumpy and bumpy. Remember this, and hook those outlines loosely, with an almost ragged quality, so that your hooked people will have a bit of life to them.

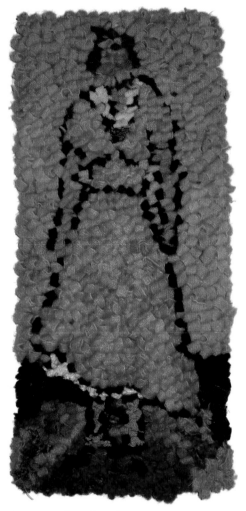

"Big Boned Girl." This woman is so different from the one on the next page. Expression is in your use of line—the slant of the shoulders or the tilt of the head.

Freehand designing of hooked people means getting good with sketching, but your sketches can be quite loose and simple. Remember, you only want to capture the idea of the person. I have asked friends

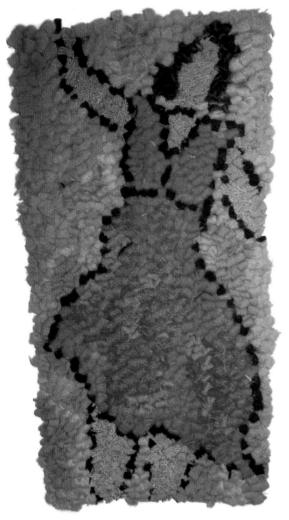

"On the Edge." I love showing spirit in my rugs. You can show it with a shaky line, like in this one.

to model for me so that I can get better at capturing gesture. I have also gone to some life modelling classes with a nude model. Drawing nudes really helps you understand body shape. When you hook people, understanding the nude body will help you see how the clothing should lie upon the body and understand the natural folds.

Clothing is the main element in hooking people. It is also the most important way you have of creating a likeness of a person. If your person is a fisherman, you will dress him as such. If he was always dressed in a suit and tie, then that is how you should hook him. If your Nan always wore an apron, then the apron you put on her will define her in a rug. When I hook clothing I outline the details of the clothing, such as collars and cuffs, a bit tighter as these are smaller and might require more definition. It is these little details that give the clothing shape, so they are important. Outlining the triangle points of a shirt and putting in a little colour for a tie makes it clear that your little man was a sharp dresser. It gives shape to the clothing. I make sure that I outline the impression of pockets and epaulettes, and highlight any small details that will enhance the clothing.

"Three Men" is an example of how to create details in clothing using different colours and outlining pockets and epaulettes.

When the clothing is hooked in large areas I will often hook two or three colours very close together to give the impression of light falling on the clothes. Several colours hooked together give the feeling of the folds that are natural as clothing drapes our bodies. You can also use a soft line of the outline colour to highlight a fold in the clothes, and to enhance the feeling of movement in your person. Patterns can be easily created in women's clothing. You can look at most patterns and recreate them on a rug. I create small floral patterns by hooking a tiny circle of pink, for example, and butting up a tiny bit of green against it. Do this in a random pattern all over the article of clothing and then hook the background in a contrasting colour and you will have a floral dress. I like to add a bit of glittery wool for earrings or a necklace on a woman. These bits do not have to be defined— just hook in a tiny bit of glittered wool and the jewelry will just emerge. I think hooking clothing is my favourite part of hooking people. The way you dress your people will tell a lot about them. I have created a series of small mats, seven by twelve inches, that I call big-boned girls. My mother always told me I was big boned. My favourite thing to do when making these little mats is choose their outfits. I did not stop playing Barbies until I was nearly fifteen, and in the last few years I've been able to do it again, in a different kind of way.

Start out hooking images of people that are not supposed to be your aunt, or sister, and move into trying to capture specific people later on.

Faces for me are not complex because with the width of wool I use I have decided that features would look cartoonish. Early on, I decided to use several shades to hook flesh tones. In larger rugs I might choose four to six shades, very close to each other in colour, but with slightly different tones under them. For a face I will start usually by hooking one of these colours in the cheek area, and another to approximate eyes and nose. When I teach people it is here that they often make a mistake. Do not hook in the shapes of eyes, nose, and cheeks. Try hooking amoeba shapes with slightly jarred edges so other colours can be butted up against these areas and blended in. Also do not hook the face as a circle to be filled in. Try to blend your colours, and use this blending to give the impression of facial features. It takes practice, and the only way you can really see the hooked impression is to step away from your mat. Distance will make the heart grow fonder.

If the faces are small, just an inch or two in diameter, you can get away with one solid colour, but it should not be hooked around and around like a circle. Try to fill the area in by hooking it jaggedly and randomly. Clip your wool and start in another area of the face rather than using one strip to fill it in completely.

I use these same techniques for all body parts. For legs and arms I hook them in long areas, and try to use the lighter shades to highlight the undersides of the arms, or the inner parts of the thighs. The non-distinct qualities that this method has lent the people in my rugs have become a kind of signature for me. I like the way they indicate commonness and a feeling that this could be anybody. I do not like many hooked rugs where facial features have been hooked towards a realistic likeness. I find the eyes are often jarring, and the other features a bit off. This is not always true of course, and I have seen some very good ones, but this is my general feeling.

Sheep's wool and fancy yarns have been my preferred choices for hooking hair. The way you hook the sheep's wool will create a type and style of hair. If you hook it high and loose, you will have big, wild, curly-looking hair. If you hook thin strands, quite low and tight, you will have hair that looks more controlled. If you want straight hair, you might find wool cloth is a better choice.

Context and background also tell a lot about the person you are hooking. It is important to consider just where you are putting the person, and make it relevant and explanatory. People rugs are story rugs in a way, and their context is part of the story. As you hook people remember that you are not trying for an exact likeness but to approximate a feeling. Start out hooking images of people that are not supposed to be your aunt, or sister, and move into trying to capture specific people later on. You can hook a few small portraits first to work up to the idea of a creative portrait. Hooking people, like all hooking, should be fun.

"Cold Winter Day" remains a favourite rug as it so clearly evokes the feeling of winter.

Winter: Worry and Wonderland

From Dark to Light

Artists wonder, and it is their own wonder that they give voice to as they make their work. At some time we all wonder, how do you get an original idea? I think most artists ponder that question, and after some time begin to understand that pondering it too deeply becomes cumbersome. You come to the conclusion that your pondering might be an impediment to the flow of your thoughts. There is a fine line between the sweet art of wonder and the narcissism of navel gazing. Thinking too hard about creativity can get in the way of being creative. What you want to do is play, read, exercise, rest, relax, and work, in no particular order, but as the mood takes you. Well, except for work, I suppose. A nice steady even flow of work, whether you work for yourself or someone else, is necessary. Work is the backbone of being good at anything, regardless of how much talent you have been graced with.

I find that routine or rote work, as dull as it might be, is good for my mind. I generally cut all the wool for my own mats, as it intersperses the creative work with busy hands and creates a light mind. Creativity is enhanced by a light mind, one that is open to the moment, seeking joy, and remaining free from worry. Worry is a huge hazard for the creative side of our minds. If our thoughts are caught up in upsetting scenarios that we create about the future, there is no room for our ideas to percolate. It is in my nature to worry, and since I was a child I have struggled with anxiety. It is mild and luckily I have been able to control it myself through exercise, self-

"Hockey Night in Nova Scotia." A lot of my winter is spent watching children play hockey, as we have maintained a backyard rink for years.

talk, and the help of my sisters and friends. I remember as a little child lying in bed under a lumpy quilt worrying if the stove was turned off, and walking downstairs to check it repeatedly before I could sleep. My mother would call out from her bed, "What are you doing?" I'd yell back, "Just checkin' the stove." She'd say, "It's off," and let me in my little ten-year-old feet pad down the stairs and check it. My mother never "problematized" things, perhaps because it was unheard of in the seventies in rural Newfoundland, but I like to believe it was also because she just did not see the need to. She was a worrier herself, sometimes with good reason, sometimes without. Some of us I guess are born with a "worry" gene. We can let it own us, or we can own it.

Last winter I was struggling with worry more than I had in years. I was adjusting to my son growing up, getting ready to get his driver's license, soon to be followed by his leaving home. But it was not just that—my mind was wandering. You can look around for all kinds of reasons and you can come up with many rationalizations for why you feel a certain way. Personally, I think focusing on the cause can be a distraction to changing the way you think, feel, and act. I decided I needed to change the way I was acting, and perhaps that would change the way I was feeling. I was having trouble staying focused on my work, or my play. My lack of focus was making me sad. I thought to myself that I needed to change things up a bit. That was not the first winter I had felt this way, but somehow that year it felt more intense. I have never been able to soothe myself with a trip south. In fact, the constant talk about resorts and lying on the beach makes me want to stay home because I have so little to add to any of those conversations. I also have little interest in going south, which makes me a winter anomaly around here. January and February in Nova Scotia are rugged months for even the lightest of hearts. My own soul is one that muses and mulls and rolls around every possible thought, from the lightest to the darkest. It is who I am. Waking up in the dark makes me cranky. Pending storms make me worry that I'll be barred in the house with my family and once they start to drive me nuts, the roads will be too bad for me to drive to town and soothe myself with a chunky Kit Kat bar. I like winter all right, as long as the roads are open and I can sleep in until eight thirty on dark mornings. When I worry, my creativity flounders. Sitting still at the mat with my own thoughts becomes something I avoid because I start thinking too much. When I am feeling good, being left alone with my thoughts is creative slush. It is time for the juices to flow and the ideas to float to the top. When I feel worried, sitting alone with the mat is free time to worry more, so I avoid it.

As New Year's Eve approached this year I began wondering if I was slipping away from myself. Deciding that I might be, I chose to join a yoga class and in mid-January I went to a meditation workshop. I started going to yoga classes three to four times a week. In the winter, my walking gets curbed a little, as I cannot always get out to walk safely because there is either ice underfoot or a plow trying to catch up with me. The yoga, with its focus on breathing and moving and stretching, and being in the moment, was a great release. I did keep walking whenever I could get out.

The meditation workshop at a retreat centre in Tatamagouche, Nova Scotia, was about sitting meditation, and taking your mind back to your breath, even when your thoughts begin to wander. We sat for hours at a time, in stillness and quiet, each of us letting our breath lead our mind. The biggest thing I learned that weekend was that I could sit still for an hour. I am not quite sure I'd ever done that before without a book. One of the themes of the weekend, which is familiar in Buddhist writing, was to begin to see your mind as a horse and you as the rider, so that you can control your thoughts, rather than letting your mind be a wild horse that is dragging you around. Now when I get a little off track I say to myself, "Ride the horse. Don't let it ride you." I have used the sitting meditation since I came home, not for an hour, but sometimes for ten or fifteen minutes just to centre myself, and it works. I use it for a few minutes now and then. It is something I have in my backpack to soothe myself.

The biggest thing I learned that weekend was that I could sit still for an hour. I am not quite sure I'd ever done that before without a book.

I vowed to continue my walking, even if it meant walking laps on the track at the local rink. It was a much-needed effort to relax a little. These were all simple solutions, and they helped a lot because they got me focusing on my breath, and my body, rather than my thoughts. I also stopped talking so much about how I was feeling. As someone who is comfortable with even the dark side of herself, I decided that I needed to be careful of blurting out my life story just because someone asked "What's up?" I did not always need to tell the truth about how I was feeling. I also got to thinking about smiling, and how when I just use my muscles to turn up the corners

My frame waits for me in my little upstairs studio. When I hook it eases tension and frees my mind.

of my lips towards my ears, this sends a signal to my brain to get over myself. Sometimes when I was walking at the track around the rink with the music of Patti Scialfa on my iPod, at about one mile in I would feel something akin to joy. It would take me a minute to recognize it, because it had become unfamiliar. One afternoon when I was surprised by joy I decided that joy is not something to be pondered, it is something to be embraced. I decided to feel it and let my thinking mind rest.

Sometimes I pray that my mind will not wander to worry and create disasters and tragedies in my head, but then I remind myself that it is because I have this vivid and active imagination that I have been able to make great rugs and create a life around it for myself. I am an artist because my mind is active and fertile, and because my imagination goes to wild and crazy places. Wishing that you could not imagine is like wishing for blindness. My father would say, "It is like flying in the face of God." I decided instead that I can own my thoughts, and when they start going in places I don't want to go, I can jump on that horse and give it some direction.

I think I was able to comfort myself out of a creative slump by being a bit more tender with myself, a bit more forgiving, by consciously deciding to think and act differently. There were days when I let myself lie on the couch and read a bad book. I know that I was not in the middle of a clinical depression, and that these ideas are not always enough, but I do believe that these techniques are always part of getting back your groove, and getting on with your creative life. It is so easy to get off course, losing our focus, and focus is such an essential part of being good at anything.

Luckily I was able to look around me, and find what I needed right in my own area. Resources are usually close at hand, but using them is another story altogether. Sometimes now when I see the woman who built the yoga studio in our downtown, I want to make a spectacle of myself and run up, and wrap my arms around her and give her a kiss for putting that lovely studio here, but because I have been doing yoga and meditation for a few months I am able to breathe, collect my thoughts, stop myself, and just smile and say, "Thank you." Then I get up on my horse and ride right out of town.

Hooking Winter

Like many people I find the winter difficult, though there are things about it I enjoy. I love the wood fire and making a pot roast on my wood stove. I enjoy the first few storms, and always settle in to hook a few mats of winter. It would never occur to me to hook snow in July, just as does not occur to me to hook swimmers in February. The seasons, as grand or treacherous as they might be, are part of my inspiration. Hooking winter means you need to get

"On the Barrens." Hooking winter is not always about hooking snow. Think of it as hooking "cold."

"Under a Stormy Sky." Skies can be very expressive. They are a big space in a rug that allows you to create mood.

the feeling of cold across your warm mat. Once you decide to hook a winter landscape you need to remember that white is not only white but it is also the shadows that fall upon it. Look for the palest shades of any colour, choose the palest blues, greens, yellows, and mauves to create shadows. These will enhance the creams, light greys, and whites you choose.

I like to find a cream or white sweater and cut it wide. Sweaters curl as you hook them and give you a nice fluffy texture. Look for textured cream or pale yarns, curly locks, merino, silks. Try anything, because texture gives dimension on a snowy landscape. Natural sheep's wool works well as a detail of fur on coats or jackets. Add details like scarves and mittens if you are hooking people in the winter landscape. Also remember that hooking winter is not just about hooking snow, but can include cold barren fields in pale greens, tans, or golds. To get the idea of snow falling, you can hook in three or four loops of white, all throughout the image. This can be done after the rest of the rug is hooked. I often choose a textured yarn for this effect.

The sky has a certain feel to it in winter. Remember to hook a winter sky. Start looking at the sky this winter and think about how it is different from the sky in spring or summer. Winter sky often has a grey tone yet remains dramatic. I always hook the wool directionally, in the shape of the landscape. Sometimes I'll use light greys or tans to show where people have walked, or paths in the snow, and mix it with creams. It is best to avoid black as an outline as it is stark against the white. I do not outline the snowy landscape unless I want it to look stylized. This can be a great effect but it steps away from realism. Always remember there are no definitive rules, but it is nice to let a snowy landscape disappear into the sky. It looks good to me without an outline, but you may see it differently.

Hooking winter is about having the right materials at hand, but it is also about feeling winter. You need to get outside, catch a few snowflakes on your tongue, make a snow angel, and then bring that back to your rug.

"Coastal Prayer Rug." The net needles are like those carved by my father. I grew up in a house where we got on our knees to pray, but I believe my father's carving was also a kind of prayer.

Prayer is a Place to Go

When I was a teenager and would come home from being out with my friends, my mother would be lying on her back on her bed, on top of her white cotton chenille bedspread with her hands folded in prayer across the upper part of her stomach, right below her breasts. Her eyes would be closed and her head tilted slightly back as if she were looking towards the crucifix that hung over her bed. Her chin would be pointed straight up into the air. I accepted that my mother had a life full of prayer. The statue of Saint Anne in her brown dress holding the baby Mary sat upon her dresser, a relic that as a child I looked up to and as a teenager I dismissed. I recognized my mother in her prayer pose in either of the bedrooms she shared with my father in the houses we lived in when I was growing up. My father's prayer was quite different. His head would sometimes be bowed into his folded hands as he sat on the bed in a translucently thin white cotton undershirt, with his hard scratchy elbows on a small desk-like table he kept near the side of his bed. His fingers would all be entwined except for the first two on his right hand which would be holding a Winston cigarette, and smoke would be curling towards the yellowed ceiling like the spirit itself.

They both knew how to pray, each in their own way. Other times I'd come in from a car ride with a bunch of friends to find my parents kneeling beside the bed together saying the rosary. Their black beads would be clicking as they raced through the "Our

"Sisters of St. Pat's." This rug was commissioned by St. Pat's Home in St. John's, Newfoundland, as a piece of art to commemorate their 100th anniversary.

Father" followed by ten Hail Marys. This would be done five times at a speed faster than any boy I knew ever drove. They could whip through the rosary towards toast and tea at a shocking speed, and if you had not said those prayers at least seventeen hundred times yourself you would have sworn they were speaking a foreign language, or perhaps had the gift of tongues. No matter how fast it was, still they prayed, and still it was meaningful. My parents knew the value of prayer and they taught me it, day in, day out. Even at times when I was sure they were off their heads, I was learning that prayer was part of a life built upon spirit, because there they were in front of me on their knees. I, in the meantime, was smoking a cigarette and curling my hair, getting ready to make a mad dash into the first car that drove up the lane. It may not have looked like what they were doing was sinking in, but it was.

I learned from them that prayer was a place you could go inside yourself. They prayed alone, and they prayed together. Prayer was used all the time. Interestingly enough, I do not ever remember us praying over a meal as a grace. Prayer was more like something you did when you had the time, like if you were driving into town to bingo. In the car we prayed, and even on the way to church we prayed sometimes. I would recite the Hail Mary as fast as my father, sometimes making a game of it to see how fast I could actually say it. Prayer was something you fit into the routine of your day, but it was also something you turned to when things were quiet and you were alone with your thoughts. For my mother and father, prayer was a response to life. I was a teenager and they were bowing heads, or looking to the sky, and I was wandering about in a seeming fog but obviously sucking it all up, because now at forty-three, with a teenage son of my own, I pray. I pray that he will be good, that he will be safe, that he will do well, and even that he will know how to pray himself. I pray that he will be kind to his sister, and wish for him all the things I know he dreams of for himself. I pray for myself that I will be a good mother when all he wants from me is a hot meal and a drive. It is not easy to be a good mother to someone who does not want a mother bothering him at all. I pray that my anxiety won't overcome my common sense and that my worry for him won't turn me into an incessant nag who twiddles and paces. Unlike my mother I don't pray to Saint Anne. I don't have a picture of Jesus in my mind, I just pray to God, and in truth I don't really know what God looks like. I just know God.

Sometimes now I read Buddhist teachers and I use their ideas to get closer to God. In doing that I realize that my parents practiced like Buddhists too. They were like some kind of Catholic Buddhists, a religion they seemed to have invented themselves. Their mantra was the "Christ have mercy," with their favourite chant being the rosary. Their meditation pose was either on their knees, flat on their back, or head bowed, smoking. When I started reading Pema Chodron and Thich Nhat Hanh, I identified with so much of

"In praise and thanks." There are so many ways to pray. Turning our heads to the sky reminds us of the need to.

it because I had already seen people live some of it, though they used different words to identify it. I grew up Catholic around nuns and priests and brothers, and went to church every week, but even as a small child the only sanctity I ever really felt in church was through the week when I would go there alone, or with another friend, and there were only one or two other people there. I remember how hollow the building felt, and how full my little nine-year-old spirit felt with the empty pews and the high ceilings with the light fixtures that had been saved from the old church in Merasheen. I used to do the stations of the cross, following the passion of Christ around the church, blessing myself, and saying prayers. I can still feel it, like the warmth of Mary's blue cloak covering me. Though I read about spirituality from all kinds of traditions, and believe there are many good truths from all cultures and traditions, I feel that I need to remain connected to the culture that spawned me because that is who I am. Sometimes other traditions seem to make more sense, but I have found that I can take those bits and incorporate them into the culture where I feel I belong.

John O'Donohue, the Irish philosopher, once wrote that he wondered why so many people felt they needed to make a spiritual journey somewhere far away when there were so many empty sacristies in our own communities that we could visit alone any day of the week, simply by asking at the office. This rings true with me. If you want to connect with the spirit, you just need to reach your hand in the air and touch it. You could be anywhere, but a nice place to do it is in any of the quiet, beautiful, empty churches that abound in our own hometowns. The Buddhist spiritual leader Thich Nhat Hanh wrote that when he first came to America, he asked a friend to show him the American Buddha, and his friend showed him a Tibetan or Vietnamese Buddha. The spiritual leader did not understand why the Americans had not found their own Buddha, their own way of being Buddhists. I immediately identified with this. For me, my spirituality is deeply

I can't identify with the statue of the Buddha the way I do with the crucifix that hung above my mother's bed. I belong to one tradition but I know there is much to learn from other traditions.

connected with my cultural heritage, as is my work, and my whole life. I need to be able to feel that I belong, yet I rely on all kinds of Buddhist teachings to try to be good, to be better. I integrate them into my own Christian traditions because it is what works for me. Even after I finish yoga, I cross myself in blessing, the way I did when I finished my prayers with my mother at bedtime. I don't need a whole new culture. I like the one I have, I just want to add a little dash to it. I can't identify with the statue of the Buddha the way I do with the crucifix that hung above my mother's bed. I belong to one tradition but I know there is much to learn from other traditions.

Spirit and prayer for me are both communal and private, but I count on the private in a way that the communal could never fill. I count on the private to sustain me, to feed me, to keep me good. The public face of my spirituality is about the sanctity of these beautiful sacred spaces that are our churches, and the need to sustain them. I also, at times, enjoy the community of church, and of praying with others. Mostly, though, I pray when I walk, when I begin to worry, and at night when I go to bed. I try to remember to pray thanks for the day when I get up in the morning, but I often get distracted by the weather or the need to make my bed, and I forget. What can I say, I am weak, and I'm a sinner, and I forget even the most important basic things about my relationship with God. I can be distracted from prayer by the certain and perfect placement of a pillow on a bed.

I think of my mother often when I pray. I think that perhaps I was the cause of her need to pray at times. I know she worried for me and sometimes did not know what to make of me. I know I got on her nerves. I know I was selfish and thoughtless. I know, because at times I remained so into my adulthood.

The place was good, the people were kind, but she knew that she was facing the end of her life and she didn't find it easy.

When my daughter was a toddler, my mother lived with me for two months because she was sick. She did not like it that much, and neither did I, but we both knew it was good for her at that time. She needed me, and I had some amends to make. We made out okay. We took to staying out of each other's way, as we had years before. She would read the paper and hook a bit on her mat, rest and pray, and that would fill her day. I worked away frenetically looking after two small children and my husband, who had walking pneumonia (an oxymoron, since you lie on the couch with it), and I hooked rugs and ran a small business from the house. I was looking after everyone and still managing to field ten phone calls a day from my six sisters and a selection of other relatives who were inquiring about either my sick husband or my frail mother. It was an exhausting winter. Every time the phone rang I rolled my eyes. Every time one of the local sisters, Donna or Joan, visited, my mother went on from her chair about how I never stopped. I never took it as a sign.

After two months my mother decided to go back to her own place. She packed up nearly all her things and went home. We were both relieved. We had made out fine, but neither of us really liked it. A few weeks after she left she called me and asked if she had left her prayer book there. I looked but could not find it. She called several more times and asked me to check her room. I did look, probably quickly, several times, but could not find it. We talked about what it looked like, but I could not place it. After she asked me about it a few times, she gave up on it, and perhaps on me. My mother lived at home for several more months, but one day in the middle of the afternoon she had a stroke. She called my sister, all disoriented. My sister called me and we went out to find her locked in her trailer struggling on the floor of her bedroom. She then spent weeks in the hospital, some of it on the brink of death in intensive care, before she began a slow recovery. She needed extra care, and together with her and my sisters, she decided to go to a level-one nursing home called White Birches. As my mother said about getting old, "There is not much here to look forward to, Deanne." I said, "Mom, they play bingo in the kitchen two nights a week." She said, "Oh for god sakes, Deanne, they play for chocolate bars." The place was good, the people were kind, but she knew that she was facing the end of her life and she didn't find it easy. My mother lived there nearly two years. We saw each other a lot and she went out with me or my sisters often.

About two years after my mother died I was cleaning out the bookcases in the spare bedroom and I found a book by Amy Dean called *Peace of Mind: Daily Meditations for Easing Stress*. Where the hell did this come from? I thought. Inside the cover it was inscribed *To Mom, Love Georgina, Christmas 1995*. Out of it fell six little cards, her prayers. There was a prayer of thanksgiving, a prayer to St. Jude (who aids in the most desperate cases), a morning prayer to St. Anne, a prayer for all souls, a mass card for Charlie Dollmont, a beloved neighbour who had died in 1989, and finally the prayer of Saint Francis of Assisi. There in that damp spare bedroom I had found her prayer book, at least two years too late for her but still in time for me. My goodness, I thought, I never knew this was her prayer book. It was not what I would have thought to look for. I quickly felt ashamed that I had not gotten it to her. I might have even seen it as I had looked and not identified it. She had never said a title, just that it was a small prayer book and that she used it every

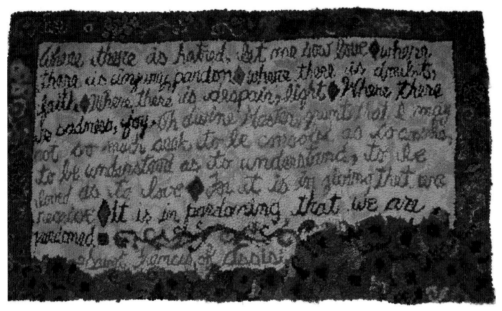

"The prayer of Saint Francis of Assisi" is one of the earliest prayers I remember learning and I continue to find it beautiful.

day. I rationalized my not finding it but at the same time I knew I had not taken the time to really listen to her, and to really look. I took the book and slid it into the drawer of my night table. It is a reminder to me to slow down, and to pray. Sometimes I use her six little prayers. Occasionally I read a passage from the book itself and try to imagine how she might have related to the little story. Mostly though, I pray in my own words. I sometimes pray with my hook. I sometimes make a mat that is a prayer. Through it all I keep the book there by my bedside as a penance, and as a reminder of things I need to know. I see it most mornings when I wake up before I head out for my walk, before I make my tea, and before I walk up the open stairs to my little studio at the back of the house.

Prayer is an escape on one level, and it is a return to the self on another. It returns us to the reality of the smallness of our lives. I saw my mother use it for both, just as I use it for both. I sometimes start to pray to deal with small worries or anxieties. It is a soothing

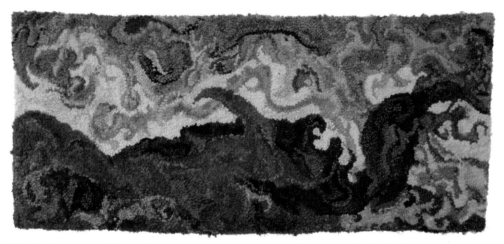

"In the Spirit." I did not draw many lines on this rug but just hooked it freely, however I felt like.

place to go. Once I get there I understand who I am in the context of my own life, and what I need to do to honour my spirit. Prayer for me is a place, and I take it with me wherever I go.

Years ago when my studio was still in the back room of my farmhouse, a rug-hooker from New Brunswick brought her mother to visit. While the daughter looked around upstairs I stayed downstairs with her mother, and worked away at bits of paperwork. The older Acadian woman was dressed very traditionally in a long wool coat, and had a bandana on her head. As she looked around she said, "Ah…dese are like the mats I had. Sure I told my daughter that." I asked her if she had hooked rugs and she said no but that her next-door neighbour had, and that she had given her one to keep by her bed. She said, "Every night I fell to my knees on that mat and said my prayers. For years I did that. It was my prayer rug, and it felt so good under my knees." It got me to thinking about the idea of prayer mats, and how many women must have used hand-hooked rugs this way. Traditionally we prayed at our bedsides, and many of our mothers and grandmothers rested their knees upon the plushness of a hooked mat. While there they prayed for the very people whose old clothes had been used to create the rug under them.

As they bowed their heads and prayed the "Our Father," they were buoyed by their sons' wool work shirts and their daughters' plaid school skirts. Their loved ones were there with them in a way. When we think of prayer rugs today we think only of the exquisitely created prayer mats that Muslims use to face Mecca as they say their prayers. Until that small Acadian woman stood in my studio, our own cultural tradition of prayer mats had never occurred to me. As she spoke I realized my own grandmother, whom I never met, had most likely bowed her own head gracefully as she bent her knees on her own hooked mats and prayed each night. It was this brief simple story, a chance encounter with that faithful Acadian woman, that inspired me to create a few prayer mats of my own.

I approached the idea a few different ways. For the first mat (page 138) I simply wrote down the prayer, of St. Francis of Assisi, surrounded it with a beautiful border, and hooked, thinking about every line of the prayer as I did it. This prayer, which I grew up with, has always been helpful and meaningful to me. It is also one of the prayers that fell out of my mother's prayer book.

In another rug I just drew out whatever shapes the spirit moved in me, and I hooked it in colours that I felt represented my spirit. This rug, "In the Spirit" (page 139), seems to me to be a rug that reflects strength and power of spirit. It is a dramatic rendition of a prayer mat. I think hooking a prayer mat is really about putting your spirit into the mat as you make it and focusing on what you are doing, knowing that you are endeavouring to create a piece of art that has spirit and strength. There are practical things you might like to consider, like using fabrics that will be soft and cozy under your knees. If you are writing words, you want to make sure that they are readable. I like to hook script in a number 6 cut, hooking it in double rows to accentuate the curves of the letters. It is also important to make sure that the colour of the script is in strong contrast to the colour of the background so that the words lift off the mat and don't fade into the background.

Hooking "Thanks and Praise," a Contemporary Prayer Rug

The design for this mat is the first rug I made in 2010, my twentieth year hooking rugs. It began, like all my designs, as an effort to make something beautiful, a prayer in itself, really. As I was making it I decided that with this rug I would create a thank-you card, and I would use it regularly to thank people for their efforts and their kindnesses. From there I thought we could give this card away in the studio to thank people for their support, and then our visitors could use it to say thank you to the people who are important in their lives. The ideas kept emerging and it became kind of a gratitude project. As I hooked at the rug, I thought that this woman with the bird in her hand was reaching out in praise of life. She was saying thank you, to God, to the universe, and to life. For me this rug is a way of saying my own prayer, one of gratitude for twenty years of doing what I love,

"Thanks and Praise." This is one of the first mats I made in the new year. It is part of my gratitude project.

for a healthy mind, body, and soul. The rug is both thanks and praise. Meister Eckhart said, "If the only prayer you ever say in your entire life is 'thank you,' it will be enough."

I decided that this rug belonged in this book as a design that readers could use and adapt for their own rug-hooking. I like to think that you might hook it as your own meditation, for yourself, or as a thank you for someone who has been good to you. You can choose your own colours (see the tips below) and can adapt the size of your design by taking the line drawing here and enlarging it as you see fit. I hooked it large as a 52-by-24-inch rug, but this pattern could be reduced to 26-by-12 easily. If you reduce it smaller than that you might want to omit the script up the side border as it will be difficult to make it readable in a smaller format. I used a number 6 and number 8 cut throughout the mat.

Outline: I used a dark plum cut in a number 6 for the outline. As this was a graphic style of rug I decided to outline the hair, face, and border to accentuate them. Sometimes I leave the face and hair not outlined to give a more natural effect.

Skin tone: I chose three shades of tan and mixed them for the skin tone in a number 8 cut. I added a bit of pink around her mouth and cheeks to give her some facial highlights.

Grass: She is standing on about twelve shades of green, cut in number 6 and 8 mixed and hooked downwards on the slant of the hill on which she is standing. I accented these wools with some hand-dyed mottled green yarns just to give a soft look to the land as she is standing in her bare feet.

Lettering: The word "thanks" is written in a heavy font to emphasize it. I outlined the letters in a strong green and filled them in shades of pink, coral, and fuchsia mixed and cut in 6 and 8. There is even a pink silk sweater hand-cut in these letters. The heavy font and outlining ensures that the words will stand out and be readable. The script up the side is also readable, but less so. It is hooked in number 8 in a strong pink colour, and the curves of the letters are reinforced by hooking a second line of the same pink cut in number 6. This keeps the curved areas of the letters from falling into the background. I also emphasized both areas of writing by making the writing and background colours (four mixed yellows and two fancy yellow yarns) in strong contrast to each other. This allows the writing to stand out off the background.

Hair: I chose five shades of brown from a walnut to a rust brown to a deep dark brown and cut some in 6 and some in 8. Mixing cuts makes rugs more interesting. I then hooked these wools in curving shapes and interlocked them together. I did not use fleece in this rug, as I often do for hair, because I did not want her to have a wild dancer look to her but to be a bit more subdued, and fleece is slightly harder to control.

Dress: The dress uses the same shades of pink as the word "thanks" below it but I have added a coral to accent it. I was also more liberal using the hand-cut silk sweater as it added a nice sheen. I hooked these colours downward in flowing shapes to accentuate the curves of her body. I hooked the flowers in first, using sari silk yarn to outline and accent the centres. I then hooked the teal flowers in a random fashion making each flower slightly different from the others to approximate how fabric might look if it were draped across your body. In the flowers I used teal cloth, some hand-dyed curly wool, and some hand-dyed slub yarn, which goes from thick to thin. I hooked the centres in mauve accented by white or yellow.

Blue Sky: This background was hooked simply, using two blue wool cloths very close in colour to each other in a number 8 cut.

Bird: This little bird is important in the rug, but it is like a discovery. You see that she is holding a little bird in her hand after looking at the overall picture. It was outlined in a dark blue and hooked in rust, using two rusts cut in number 6 and variegated yarn to give a feathered effect.

their praises sung

People like you deserve to have their praises sung

THANKS